Eating Heaven
Spirituality at the Table

Simon Carey Holt

ACORN PRESS

Published by Acorn Press Ltd, ABN 50 008 549 540

Office and orders:
PO Box 282
Brunswick East
Victoria 3057
Australia
Tel/Fax (03) 9383 1266
International Tel/Fax 61 3 9383 1266
Website: www.acornpress.net.au

© Simon Carey Holt 2013

National Library of Australia Cataloguing-in-Publication entry:

Author:	Holt, Simon Carey, 1962– author
Title:	Eating heaven: spirituality at the table / Simon Carey Holt
ISBN:	9780987428639 (paperback)
	9780987428646 (ebook)
Subjects:	Eating (Philosophy)
Dewey Number:	641.01

Apart from any fair dealing for the purposes of private study, research, criticism or review, no part of this work may be reproduced by electronic or other means without the permission of the publisher.

Unless otherwise indicated, Scripture quotations are taken from the New Revised Standard Version Bible, copyright © 1989 by the Division of Christian Education of the National Council of the Churches of Christ in the USA and are used by permission. All rights reserved.

Cover design: Andrew Moody, Blackburn VIC.
Text design and layout: Communiqué Graphics, Lilydale VIC.
Printed by: Openbook Howden Design & Print, Adelaide SA.

To my mother

Marie Winifred Peta Sue

Table of Contents

Preface		vii
1	An Introduction Eating and Spirituality	1
2	The Kitchen Table Eating, Identity and Formation Recipe: *Mum's Chocolate Pudding*	9
3	The Backyard Table Eating, Sustainability and Suburbia Recipe: *Vietnamese Coleslaw*	25
4	The Café Table Eating, Sidewalks and Community Recipe: *Double Chocolate and Cranberry Brownies*	43
5	The Five-star Table Eating, Beauty and Justice Recipe: *Raspberry and White Chocolate Pavlova*	61
6	The Work Table Eating, Cooking and Vocation Recipe: *Anna's Baumkuchen*	79
7	The Festive Table Eating, Celebrating and Mourning Recipe: *Lasagne for Sharing*	97
8	The Multicultural Table Eating, Culture and Inclusion Recipe: *Sinh Khein's Spring Rolls*	113
9	The Communion Table Eating, Sacrament and Connection Recipe: *Credo's Zucchini Slice*	131
10	Conclusion Eating Heaven	147
References and Further Reading		151

Preface

I can only hope this book is easier to read than it was to write. Though I have wrestled with its words for a string of years, I have been pinned to the mat and unable to move more times than I can count. The challenge has not been so much my inability to write as beautifully as I imagine one should. Thankfully my aspirations for writing are much humbler than they once were. The challenge is more to do with the subject of the book and the question of its merit.

The act of eating is a troubled business; to write about it is fraught. I've spent too much of my time in food's shadow, professionally and otherwise, to view it romantically. For the most part, table life speaks of monotony and ordinariness, and at its more refined edge, decadence and excess. Surely the investment demanded by good writing could be more profitably targeted to a subject matter that really matters. Or so the conversation in my head goes.

Routinely, though, I have been prodded to think again, and it is this prodding that has kept me at the keyboard. Marion Halligan, one of Australia's most intelligent food writers, is a wise and moderating voice in what can be a pompous genre. For Halligan, eating is a conversation, a relationship, a way of being in everyday life. Its beauty is its simplicity, its ability to bring us together, and its connection to the earth's rhythms and seasons. In a long-forgotten essay from the 1970s, Halligan critiques the style and approach of food writing in the Australian press. Part way through she says this:

> Writing about food is not a totally satisfactory activity. It has too many intimations of decadence, in a world where so often the mere presence of food is such an event that the consideration of its elegance would be an obscenity. The only justification of our preoccupation with food is that, since we do eat a great deal, we should do it well.

It is Halligan's exhortation to 'do it well' that has kept me struggling for words that take eating seriously; words that treat our life at the table as the significant thing it is. According to Halligan, to eat well is not to eat extravagantly, but to do so mindfully, respectfully and justly. Indeed, in this age of culinary infatuations, global food crises, celebrity chefs and Biggest Losers, the need to reflect more seriously upon eating is pressing. It is this idea of eating well – eating as a spiritual act – that I have tried to explore.

Writing is a solitary business, yet a book is never written alone. I am indebted to the people who have journeyed with me through this book's living and writing. To those who hosted my earliest, stumbling days in the professional kitchen, especially Graeme and Anna, I owe more than I can name. I came alive in their kitchens in a way I had never been before. I only wish I had the insight at the time to tell them. To those who have submitted to formal interviews and informal conversations around the subject of this book, those whose stories appear in its pages and those that inform it: thank you. To the congregation at Collins Street that has allowed me such generous leave for writing, and especially my colleague Carolyn Francis who has stepped in with such competence: thank you. To Philip and Stuart, my gracious hosts at Clevedon Manor in Castlemaine where I've found a home to write these past three years: thank you. To the team at Acorn Press, especially my cheerleaders Rena Pritchard and the late John Wilson and my editor Kristin Argall, who have graciously and patiently encouraged me in the writing process: thank you. And to my dear friend Dianne Brown, the person who has so consistently embodied what this book is about and lives a life at the table that gathers so many others into its sphere of grace. Without knowing her influence, she has inspired me with the most tangible reminders that this business of eating is important far beyond what's on the plate. Thank you, Di.

I am deeply grateful to my family, my children Ali and Nathaniel and my wife Brenda. Not only have these three allowed me to feed them these past two decades, they have shared a table and a home with me, absorbed my weariness and forgiven my imperfections, inspired my writing, and kept me grounded in the most ordinary wonder of life. What's more, without logic or reason Brenda's confidence in me has never failed.

Finally, this book is dedicated to my mother who at the time of publication has just celebrated her eightieth birthday. My own life at the table is so intimately tied to her: her love, self-giving, faith and unfailing optimism. Cooking has never been Mum's first love, not even her second or third. Her faith in God has always been first in her life, as have been the people, so many people, whom she believes God brought her way. Whatever energy and time she has invested at the stove, more years than I can know, she has given out of love. I am forever in her debt.

Simon Carey Holt
Melbourne

CHAPTER 1

An Introduction
Eating and Spirituality

This morning I had eggs for breakfast. It's a Friday ritual and I am a creature of habit. After making coffee for my beloved and sitting with her to breathe the quiet morning air, I shower and dress, wake my two children, pack their lunches and make them breakfast. Cajoling them out the door on a Friday is more challenging than usual, but eventually they depart. My beloved follows close behind. Once they've all left, I leave too. It's on my way to the market, another Friday routine, that I stop in at a local café for my ritual meal: poached eggs on sourdough with mushrooms, and a strong flat white.

Though my café of choice is not as hip as others close by, it's a comforting place as a café should be, one with a feeling of intimate yet open space and a view of the cobbled pedestrian laneway out the front. Each week I sit at the same table, a long communal one of dark and solid wood surrounded by stools. I nod and smile at those around me. Occasionally we chat. In a simple and momentary way we are bound by this shared object and space. The waiter is a young woman, Australian-born of Japanese descent. Warmly as always, she greets me by name. If it's available, I read the morning paper. If it's taken, I revert to the book I've brought with me. It's a simple meal in an ordinary place, but I've come to value that half-hour ritual as a spiritually significant one; as significant and sustaining, in fact, as any routine practice of my life.

Eating is a sacred business. Whether it's eggs on toast in a café, cornflakes scoffed down at the kitchen bench, a sandwich shared with colleagues in the cafeteria, or a leisurely family dinner at the dining room table, eating is a spiritual act. Granted, to define eating in this way has the sound of wistful nonsense. Indeed, sitting down at a table to eat is an activity so grounded in the ordinary, so basic to the daily routines of life, we rarely ponder it beyond the simple inquiry, 'What's for dinner?' However, scratch a little deeper and you discover in eating one of the most meaning-laden activities of our lives, one so immersed in human longing and relationship that it's a practice of sacred dimensions.

This is a book about eating and the tables of daily life that play host to it. It's a personal book; it arises out of my own story. I am a product of the table. Raised in a close-knit, working-class home of father, mother and a busload of sons on the suburban edge of Melbourne, my most enduring memory is of family life around the table. I recall sitting there night after night, year after year – the food, the laughter, the arguments, the stories and prayers; all so mundane, but formative in profound ways.

I am a trained chef. With my father's encouragement I left high school to begin my apprenticeship in the kitchen. Though my career was never salubrious, it was life giving. I felt at home in the kitchen in ways I had never felt elsewhere. Through the specialties of pâtissier and garde-manger, I found the most wonderful avenues for the creativity that had simmered internally for so long. Though my culinary career is now past, my passion for food – its beauty, variety and endless possibility – endures as a defining aspect of who I am.

I am a person of faith. In fact, I am a minister of religion, engaged professionally in understanding and communicating what it is to seek meaning and transcendence in life. I cannot avoid the formative influence the Christian faith has had upon my life and my view of the world, nor do I wish to. Though in writing this book I have no particular barrow to push – this is not a veiled attempt to proselytise the reader – I am intrigued by what's going on in the deepest part of who we are, individually and communally, when we sit down at the table to eat. And I am intrigued by the growing interest among people all across Australia in nurturing a synergy between what they eat and what they value.

I am a teacher, a lecturer in a tertiary institution, and a researcher in urban sociology and spirituality. For the last fifteen years I have been exploring with students – those from a range of religious and non-religious backgrounds – what it means to live with an awareness of the sacred in everyday life. What's more, I am fascinated by the role food plays in any society as an expression of culture and a maker of meaning. I read far too much about the history, anthropology, sociology and psychology of eating.

I am a husband and a father, a primary carer and cook for my small family. I make breakfasts, pack lunches and prepare dinners day after day. We eat in as a family and invite others to join us. We eat out, enjoying the delights of a wonderfully diverse city. In the midst of all of this, I have a growing sense that the tables of everyday life, whether in or out, are potentially holy places, altars at which sacred transactions take place.

Whether from an overtly religious perspective or not, it's important that we value what takes place at our tables, finding ways to embrace them more intentionally and intelligently than we presently do. It is this conviction that motivates the writing of this book. In an age of fast food, microwave ovens and fragmented schedules, the dining room table sits routinely empty in many households, a museum-like tribute to a quaint practice of long ago. Indeed, times have changed and so much of life has improved along the way. But what has been lost? The quest for meaning, intimacy and community seems ever more urgent. The table beckons. It beckons because, at its core, the table is about such fundamentally human things as intimacy and family, identity and communication, reconciliation and romance, covenant and community, redemption and friendship, sustenance and celebration, beginnings and endings. The table beckons because it plays host to so much more than biological necessity.

Of course, the basic proposition of this book is a troubling one. As a religious professional, I know how fraught it is to propose eating as a spiritual activity. Even among those who share my religious inclinations, perhaps even more so, enfolding something as routine as eating into one's moral or religious framework is an awkward embrace, and for good reason. There are yellow lights that flash caution.

Firstly, eating has traditionally held a suspect place in religious conversation. Initiate a discussion around eating in a Christian context and two words commonly rise to the surface: *gluttony* and *fasting* – one the sin of doing it too much and the other the spiritual virtue of not doing it at all. One is left with the impression that eating is, at best, a spiritually neutral activity and, at worst, a downright hindrance to deeper pursuits.

Secondly, for many people, eating is tied to so much that is painful and spiritually destructive in human experience. The prevalence of eating disorders like anorexia and bulimia are tragic reminders of this. In a society obsessed with Biggest Losers, body image and a never-ending stream of faddish diets and celebrity waifs, food is increasingly judged the enemy to self-acceptance. Consequently, addressing eating as a spiritual act is a tough call.

Thirdly, when we look honestly at the international table, we can't ignore the tragic inequity of food distribution throughout the world. We watch the evening news, shifting uncomfortably in our seats as we see children in far-off places with distended tummies and sunken eyes. While we endlessly graze, these children are dying through lack of the most basic nutrition. The injustices of our world are no more graphically displayed than at the global table, where the rich feast endlessly while the poorest sit on the floor hoping desperately for some crumbs to fall their way. All very well for those of us who live in places of plenty to describe eating as a spiritual act, to make food a fetish only because we've never known its lack. Frankly, it can sound too much like the self-indulgent claptrap of consumerist spirituality that pervades our well-padded lives.

Fourthly, and perhaps most immediately, the dynamics of ordinary life makes dinnertime in the average home feel anything but spiritually profound. Sitting any household down to the intimate proximity of the

An Introduction

table at the end of a long day is a hazardous move. First, simply finding it under the pile of domestic debris that gathers can be challenge enough. Once seated, what happens there can be loaded. Rather than a site for elegant repose and uplifting conversation, the dinner table can morph into a battleground; the venue for disagreements, heated negotiations, frayed tempers and raised voices. The clashing of wills over uneaten vegetables, arguments over who does the dishes and who did them last, and the constant reminders of the generational gaps and power struggles that mark most households are all sobering reality checks. It can make one cynical about an overly romanticised view of the shared table.

These challenges acknowledged, it remains my conviction that the table is sacred space and that what we do there is spiritually significant. I do not cling on to this notion in spite of the aforementioned yellow lights but precisely because of them. For each one illustrates not the spiritual poverty of eating, but its potency. What we do at the table expresses most tangibly what we believe, what we value and how we understand ourselves in relation to the world around us. In the words of theologian L. Shannon Jung, food today is 'a cultural, spiritual, and moral casserole'. Indeed, eating is a social and political act of profound consequence, one that expresses tangibly our community identity and citizenship. And as one of the most routine activities of life – one that marks the rhythm and flow of every day – eating is embedded at the heart of what it means to be human.

To explore this spirituality of the table, I invite you to sit with me for a while at a number of tables, those that commonly play host to our experience of food. We begin at the kitchen table, the place where our earliest identity is shaped, manners learned, tastes and prejudices inherited, and our understanding of interdependence begins. It's a significant table of formation, a place of intimacy and power that is both constructive and destructive and everything in between. From there we move outdoors to the backyard table, the place of vegetable gardens, beer and barbecues, and the most local expression of culture. It's a table laden with far more than sausages and coleslaw, one that embodies our shared and overwhelmingly suburban view of the world and each other. Next we'll sit at the café table, the one that has mushroomed on the pavements of our cities and suburban shopping strips; a table that plays host to the city in community and to our common aspirations for the good life. Then it's indoors again to the more exclusive five-star table reserved for those who can afford it, the one set with white linen and wine glasses; a table that feeds our in-built need for beauty while dividing society's 'haves' and 'have-nots' in ever clearer ways. From there we travel the short distance from the restaurant dining room to its kitchen, the work table where the chefs, waiters and dishwashers vie for space, recognition or just a decent wage; the one where dreams of recognition, success, even celebrity, simmer as relentlessly as the stock. Next stop is the festive table, the one at which we mark, grieve and celebrate the significant moments of life: the beginnings and endings; the celebrations and losses; the transitions, accomplishments and disappointments. It's then on to the multicultural table, one that embodies the diversity of our communities and all that binds us together; and one that just as easily highlights the cultural gulfs that mark the eating landscape of our cities. Finally, we'll sit for a while at the communion table, that more explicitly religious one that sits at the centre of churches like mine. For some, this will be a familiar table and for others a foreign and uncomfortable place. Regardless, whether we remain there or not, it's one that helps us better understand why all tables are spiritually charged, rich with possibility for all people regardless of tradition or belief.

My Friday morning eggs were overcooked today, not the perfectly formed whites and deliciously runny yolks I've come to expect. There was someone new in the kitchen I noticed, and I was irritated. As I poked my fork discontentedly around my plate, the elderly gentleman across the table asked me to pass the sugar. He is there most Friday mornings in his three-piece suit that looks almost as old as he does. A perfectly folded handkerchief protrudes from his top pocket. We have spoken briefly on many occasions, enough for me to know that he has come out of retirement to assist his son in the setting up of his own legal practice, but not enough to know his name. He often looks tired, but today the weariness was marked.

'How are you this morning?' I asked.

'Yes, well thank you,' he responded in his usual polite and deliberate way, 'just a little tired. It is Friday!'

'Hmm,' I answered, looking at him, reminded again of my own grandfather who had passed away years before. Though Grandad was a farmer, tall and lean – so different in stature and profession to this elderly, small-of-frame, urban solicitor – the lines on their faces were remarkably similar and tone of voice so very much the same.

To be honest, café conversations are never easy for me to navigate. Finding the right balance between interest and interference is a juggling act that requires more wisdom than courage. Not an extravert by nature, I often remain on the more distant side of the line, but today I prodded just a little more.

'The business going well?' I asked.

'Oh yes,' he said, looking down at his bowl of muesli with yoghurt and poached fruit. He was as routine in his order as I was in mine. 'But not so good for my son,' he continued after a moment's silence, 'His wife has just left him ... left him with the boys. It's all very sad.'

'I am so sorry,' I responded, putting down my knife and looking more intently at him. 'I am so sorry.'

'Thank you,' he said, returning the gaze. 'I'm sorry too.'

We pushed our cutlery around on our plates for some long moments. It was not an awkward silence. It felt more like an appropriate one, until, without looking up, I said, 'You never stop being a dad, do you?'

'No, you certainly don't,' he said. 'I lie awake now just as much as I ever did when he was a boy.'

'I bet you do,' I replied, looking up at him again.

'Still, life goes on, doesn't it?' he said, exhaling deeply as he lifted the teaspoon from his coffee. 'Life goes on.'

As my old friend went back to reading his paper and I returned more intentionally to my eggs, their overcooked state didn't seem as important as it had those few minutes ago. As I had thought to myself so many times before, eating is never just about the food. More often than not, eating is the lubricant that makes so many other things possible.

CHAPTER 2

The Kitchen Table
Eating, Identity and Formation

Kitchen tables are carriers of memory. While they provide a place for our crockery and glassware and a convenient setting to eat, they also hold our sense of self; they tell us who we are. It's certainly true of mine. Though the kitchen table of my childhood is long gone, I can still recall it in all its flat and mundane detail. I would love to sit at it again, to feel it with both hands, but I can't. What I feel when I recall it, though, is as tangible as any object could be.

To claim it as a dining room table would be more aspiration than truth. The family home was small, too small for a room dedicated to dining alone. I grew up in a large family – Mum, Dad and six boys – in a home of just eleven squares. Each night we crowded into three bedrooms and each evening we gathered around the kitchen table.

The table stood in a small space one side of the kitchen bench beside a curtained window with a view of the driveway and a high paling fence. In today's home it might be a 'meals area', separate from the more formal dining room. For our family it's all there was. The table was oblong, veneered in a brown faux-wood laminate; very 1970s with slim and slightly angled cast-iron legs. Around it were the chairs, eight of them covered in leather-look vinyl. The vinyl changed colours over the years. With a penchant for interior decoration, my mother did all she could with limited resources to ensure our eating space remained fashionable, in a working-class sort of way. The chairs began white, as I recall, then orange. Mum says there were no other colours but these, but I'm sure there were. In my memory the chairs changed colour as often as the wallpaper. But that's another story.

While the table was cleared and set for dinner each night – usually my job – it was much more than an eating place. During the day the kitchen table served as a workbench, the hub of operations in the housekeeping department. It was the utility bench for sorting and folding laundry, a sewing table where Mum made curtains or mended trousers, and the landing place for the endless bags of groceries unloaded from the car. For years my mother was part of a neighbourhood food co-op, though well before the name for it existed. In reality it was a small group of friends who did a fortnightly run to the buy-in-bulk warehouse and loaded up their cars with oversized tins, boxes and bags of everything imaginable. They would return to headquarters – our kitchen table – where everything was measured, weighed and divided according to need. Where on earth in that small house my mum stored all these things, I still don't know. I do remember an oversized chest freezer appearing on the back porch and my oldest brother Mark building a floor-to-ceiling cupboard in the laundry with sliding louver doors. Looking in there once or twice, I thought we must be stocking up for the possibility of some religious Armageddon. Given my family's distinct religious leanings, such possibilities were always on the horizon. To a young boy raised on fire-and-brimstone preaching, this overstocked cupboard was comforting in an odd sort of way. We were ready.

The table was also a place for daily conversation, a place for copious cups of tea as friends and neighbours dropped in for a chat, and the venue for late-night meetings of the co-conspirators who, with my parents, were the pillars of the local Baptist church. Even more, it was the place where weary heads were rested at the end of long school days, one where Mum would perch herself, tea towel over her shoulder, as though she had all the time in the world to sit, talk, probe and listen. Mostly probe. There was never anything more important to Mum than people, and her boys were high on the list. Gregarious, determined, eternally optimistic and generous to a fault, she has loved so easily, so much and for so long, that the lines marking her face today speak deeply of a lifetime of love and self-giving. The table was her counselling bench, her listening post. It was also where she hatched plans, endless and optimistic plans mostly to do with money. Each week as my dad handed over his pay packet, Mum would sit at the table scribbling budgets into notepads, her tongue working double time as it moved in unison with her pen. As she schemed and manoeuvred, shifting payments from one week to the next, moving ten dollars from this column to that, she somehow managed to ensure her family had everything it needed for the week to come.

With dishes cleared away, the table was the place for homework. With none of us beset with great academic aspirations, the disciplines of study were foreign to the Holt boys and remained that way for the most part. My parents did their level best to keep us seated at the table for as long as possible, books open, blank pieces of paper staring up at us and pens twiddling in our fingers. But all to no avail. I remember my brother Greg, never one for the written word, sitting at the table from dinnertime to bedtime, set with the task of writing a short essay on this or that. As Mum finally shuffled him off to bed, his page stood blank except for the identifying words 'Greg Holt' scrawled in the top corner.

Late at night, the table could become a place of arbitration, one where Mum and Dad would sit with one of their boys found guilty of a misdemeanour of some sort – of which there were many – and negotiate the consequences. Wisely, my parents kept such interactions confidential as far as they could, hence the hour at which they happened. As far as I recall, I was never summoned to that particular table. I was too compliant, too dull to risk anyone's wrath let alone that of my parents, but my older brothers were not so constrained. Consequently, I remember on occasion lying in bed and hearing the muffled sounds of tense voices, pleas of innocence and tears. But before and after it was anything else, the kitchen table was a place to eat.

Looking back, the dinner table must have been a tight squeeze, but I was not conscious of it. It all felt very normal, and in my memory, a place I identify easily with what it means to be family. We all had our places at that table: my father at one end; Mum to his right; Mark the eldest at the counter end; and the rest of us fanned out in between. I was number five of the six boys. My younger brother Ben did not arrive until I was eleven years old, so for my first decade or so there was one seat spare, routinely offered to a visitor or one of the many girlfriends who came and went with the years.

When I think of family, I think most easily of two things: our annual summer camping holiday at the beach and our daily meals at the kitchen table. Why these? I suspect because they had as much to do with our togetherness as a family as anything else. While the rest of life was busy, fragmented – every member peeling off in different directions each day – it was on holidays and at the table we were together. In these two places we were more family than we were anywhere else.

As it happens, the most vivid memories I have of those annual camping trips are to do with food. We had one of those retractable camping tables, the nifty sort that folds up neatly into a carry case complete with handle. Set up under the awning of the tent, it only had four seats, so the rest of us would sit on folding chairs scattered about and balance plastic plates on our knees.

Holiday fare was not gourmet. My mother, who did not delight in cooking at the best of times, looked for the cheapest and easiest options available. After all, this was her holiday too. Perhaps some sausages grilled on the barbecue, or a can of camp pie, a meat substance that looked more like dog food than something for human consumption. Removed from the can, it would be cut into thick slices, seared on both sides in a frypan and camouflaged with liberal doses of tomato sauce. This would be accompanied most commonly by a saucepan full of Surprise Peas – dehydrated little nuggets that came ready for water in a small foil packet – and a generous heaping of Deb Instant Mashed Potato, a powdery substance that had only to be mixed with water and a little butter and, hey presto, mashed potato just liked Mum made at home … only different. I liked it.

The treats for the day were my favourite. After our early morning swim, Mum handed around the Arnott's Assorted Cream Biscuits for morning tea. We didn't get creamed biscuits at home, only plain ones; they were too expensive apparently. But on holidays, hang the expense! Mum bought the largest possible tin she could find and doled them out, one at a time according to a strict daily ration. Of course, when she was not looking we would sneak into the tent and take a second, even a third. Each year she was genuinely perplexed by the speed at which the tin emptied. In the afternoon, it was an Icy Pole from the local campground store. This sweet, mid-afternoon, melt-in-your-mouth-and-drip-down-your-chin frozen delicacy was definitely the highlight of those long and languid days.

Back from holidays, the nightly menu was reasonably standard for a home and budget like ours. Mum was certainly not a fussy cook, nor a woman particularly invested in her kitchen identity, but she worked hard at providing nutritious, substantial and, as far as possible, interesting meals. The more I know her as an adult, the more I understand the burden it was to her. 'If I never had to cook another meal again ...' she often says today, trailing off into nothing as though the sentence finishes itself. After all the cooking she has done in her life – an act of love more than creativity – I cannot fault her for that. In fact, if ever we go to my parents' home for dinner today, I cook; it's the least I can do.

My memory says that we had mashed potatoes every night of my childhood, accompanied by an alternating offering of peas or beans resurrected from the freezer, and some other generally overcooked vegetable on the side. Lamb chops were common, as were ham steaks, black pudding, tuna casserole, corned beef with white sauce, or the slightly exotic curried sausages served over rice with a fistful of sultanas mixed in. There was the weekly roast dinner – usually lamb with roasted potatoes, assorted vegetables and gravy. Apart from parsnip that Mum understood as essential to a roast – a priority that I could not understand and still don't – this was surely one of the most iconic and comforting meals we ate. To this day I cannot reproduce it, no matter how hard I try. It may well have to do with the absence of dripping, but perhaps the recollected flavour of a meal like this is more to do with memory than reality.

Dessert was served every night without fail, occasionally tinned fruit with cream or ice-cream, but more often a baked dessert of some kind – bread-and-butter pudding, apple pie, jam sponge, and Mum's all-time signature dish, chocolate pudding – a simple blancmange made on the stovetop, poured into dessert bowls and set in the refrigerator. Occasionally, for a slightly up-market variation, Mum would sprinkle desiccated coconut on the top, but I preferred it au naturel. With eyes wide, our smiles broadened as Mum placed the chilled bowls before us. We took turns pouring thickened cream straight from the plastic bottle all over the top, followed by generous spoonfuls of sugar to ensure maximum impact. Endless scraping of spoons around the bottom of the bowls was followed by the licking ritual. Spoons discarded and hands clasping the bowls' sides, our faces disappeared behind them, heads bobbing up and down, the most atrociously delicious sounds emanating from every place at the table. Though deemed an unacceptable practice at any other time, Mum seemed to turn a blind eye to it when it came to chocolate pudding, perhaps because Dad's head was in his bowl first. It was heaven for us all.

Of course, meal times at the kitchen table were not only about the food. I come from a family of storytellers. Though it's never been my strong point – the well-practised listener of the family – there are others who relish a good story, exaggerating shamelessly at every opportunity. Interestingly, it was always after dinner that the stories flowed. With the plates scraped clean, somehow the table gave its own permission for conversation to flourish. The English writer Elizabeth Luard observes this as a near-universal rule of the table. 'When the belly is full,' she says, 'the heart can roam.'

In reality, the stories we told were few in number but voluminous in the telling. And no matter how many times they were told, we loved them as our own. Stories defined us; they signalled our belonging, our connections, our identity as a family unit. There was a liturgical movement to these stories, as though one led naturally to another. The sense of shared expectation was expressed in rolled eyes as though we despaired of our own predictable litany, yet nobody moved. The same punch lines, the same sequences – get things out of line and the corrections were quickly made. We laughed a lot at that table, and through the telling and retelling of our stories we cemented a shared identity that remains with us to this day.

But it was not all stories and laughter. The table was also a place for tensions, disagreements and tears; usually mine. As son number five, I was a quiet boy and wretchedly sensitive. Tears were my enemy, uncontrollable and always bubbling just under the surface, ready to roll at a moment's provocation. 'Sook' was the word I came to fear the most; a tag of weakness; an indication of my failure as a man-in-training. I hated my tears; I hated my soft heart. I longed to be strong and resilient, full of bravado and indifference. I remember lying in bed at night practising my clever comeback lines, but all to no avail. Growing up in a family of men, one learned that tears were unmanly; tears were weakness; tears were feminine; at worst a manipulative wile, an expression of power for those who could find it no other way. I watched closely my father's response to my mother's tears, as occasional as they were, and understood early on this display of emotion was not the path to masculine success.

Inevitably things were said at the table that were harsh, unintended perhaps, and in retrospect, mostly harmless. But it only took a word, a criticism, a look, a kick under the table, and my tears flowed. I would leave the table quickly to rolled eyes and impatient sighs. Sitting alone in the bathroom, as frustrated with myself as I was hurt by others, I would sob quietly until, inevitably, Mum arrived to coax me back to the table. I would return to the table, conscious of male disapproval all round. Dad would never come to the bathroom, only Mum. I felt his disappointment, his impatience with this weakness of character too often on show.

Is all this really so? I don't know. Memory is an oddly selective but powerful thing. It shapes us; it gives form to the way we understand ourselves. For me these table experiences were crucial to my self-appraisal and, therefore, to my development. In truth, my relationship with the men of my family is one of the good gifts of my life. I could not ask for a kinder, gentler or more gracious father than the one I have, and have always had. But perhaps it's true that the family story, from generation to generation, weaves its way through the family line at the table. Dad grew up on a wheat and sheep farm in the Mallee of northern Victoria. He was only six years old when he lost his mum. Though my grandfather was a good and loving man, the environment was harsh and unforgiving. The character traits of resilience, physical and emotional, were crucial. Perhaps this aversion to tears was propagated here. Wherever it began, its influence remains.

A few years back, sitting at my own kitchen table with my wife and two children, we were devouring a meal of homemade tacos. It was a build-your-own adventure: taco shells, spicy mince, diced tomatoes, shredded lettuce, sour cream and grated cheese all set out on the table. I watched as my son, seated beside me, piled up the ingredients into his overflowing shell and then, with both hands, navigated the whole creation toward his mouth. Just as it arrived, the ingredients fell everywhere, a great avalanche of food falling as if in slow motion to the table and the floor around it. Instinctively we all laughed, all except my son. Out of the blue, he dropped whatever remained onto the plate below, began hitting his palm against his forehead, and with hot tears streaming down his face repeated over and over again, 'I'm so stupid! I'm so stupid!' The power of his emotion and the flood of tears caught me completely off guard; I was immobilised. I had no idea what to do. I did nothing but stare in disbelief. It took my wife at the other side of the table to get up out of her seat, come to my son's side and put her arm around his shoulder to comfort and reassure him. Why could I not do that as instinctively as she did? He was seated right next to me. Why, given my own history, did I sit there and do nothing? I don't know, but as I have reflected often on those questions, I have a hunch that the influence of tables past play a role I've yet to fully understand.

The kitchen table of my boyhood was also a religious place. On weekdays, our evening meal ended in the same way each night. My father would remove from the bookshelf a large, black, soft-covered Bible and read to us, most commonly a story from the Old Testament. Full of the most intriguing and sometimes bloody stories, the Old Testament was, according to Dad, a much more interesting prospect for young boys than the more gentle parables of the New Testament. At the end of the story, Dad would say something about its moral teaching, prod us with a question or two, and then, finally, lead us to pray. Our heads bowed and in respectful silence, we listened as each person at the table mumbled their way through a prayer of some sort.

All of this was such a standard practice in our home that I never thought to question it, nor even to dread or resent it. In fact, it's true that I learned far more about the Christian faith at that family table than in all of the tedious Sunday School classes I endured as a boy. So much so, I tried very hard to replicate the experience with my own children. When they were small, I bought a big black Bible of my own and stowed it conveniently on the sideboard. When the meal was over I reached for the sacred book and proceeded to instruct my two budding believers. But it was a dismal failure. As I read, both children would squirm endlessly in their seats, argue, kick each other under the table, ask far too many questions, and cast serious doubt on the veracity of every story I told. And that's before I even tried to pray. Honestly, it was a disaster from beginning to end. Here I was a clergyman, a so-called expert in religious formation, and I could not even teach my own children to pray. Even grace before the meal, something I've managed to maintain through the years, has had its dubious moments. When the children were young, we decided on the strategy of having a candle in the middle of our table that we would light at the beginning of the meal. After lighting it, we would say in unison to God and each other, 'Welcome to our table!' Though my candle still burns at every meal today, wax-submerged fingers and burnt napkins are all too common. So much for the holy!

It's undoubtedly true that I learned so many things at that brown laminate table of my youth: how to be a family; how to be man, or how not to be perhaps; how to serve and how to listen; how to be in close proximity to people; how to negotiate relationship when relationship is fraught. I learned my place in the family story and claimed my place in the family line. I understood my religious tradition and was shaped as a person of faith in a particular way. I learned taste and manners, the appropriateness and otherwise of certain behaviours. I learned prejudices and formed cultural assumptions, some of which have been hard in the unlearning. To a significant degree, I am who I am because of my life at that table.

To claim the kitchen table as a formative place, a place at which identity is shaped, is not to surrender to a nostalgically romantic picture of family life: the circa 1950s one with mother in her apron and perfectly coiffed hair, father standing ready to carve the Sunday roast, and the happy and well-groomed children looking on eagerly from their seats. Such images, no matter how we update them, say more about our longings than reality. To speak of the table's role in our formation is rather to acknowledge its intimate daily-ness and therefore its power. As with intimacy, power can be positive in its impact or negative in the most destructive ways. More often, the formative power of the table is a mix of the two.

As a young minister-in-training, I was assigned to a fledgling church on Melbourne's outer suburban edge. Jennifer was part of the congregation, a young married woman with two small children. Her home was small but comfortable and well kept. Jennifer enjoyed her roles as mother, wife and neighbour and found great security in the sense of belonging she felt in her community. There was an endearing gentleness to her presence, matched by a vulnerability in the way she carried herself and related to those around her.

I noticed in my visits to Jennifer that there were pictures in her home of her husband's family, many of them on the sideboards and shelves that lined her living room, but just one solitary picture of her mum and nothing more of her own family. As we got to know one another, Jennifer would tell me snippets of her story and gradually the pain she bore from her childhood became clear.

One day over tea, as Jennifer held the picture of her mother, she told me of her mother's lifelong struggle with mental illness. She was often bedridden or hospitalised for long periods of time. Jennifer's father did not cope well with his wife's illness and became progressively more abusive toward his children, verbally and physically, most especially during Jennifer's teenage years. The time of the evening meal was the time Jennifer feared most. As the oldest of four children, it was Jennifer's task to prepare the evening meal each night. Her father expected the meal to be on the table when he arrived home from work. Invariably, Jennifer told me, the meal would be late because of the more immediate needs of her younger siblings as they arrived home from school. Night after night, no matter how hard she tried, her father would express angry disappointment in her efforts. Routinely he would berate her as 'lazy' and 'stupid'. 'You are just like your mother!' he would yell as the younger children cowered in their seats. Too often his anger resulted in physical attacks, the pain of which still bought tears to Jennifer's soft face.

All of this was now many years past. Jennifer's father was now dead and her mother permanently institutionalised. Jennifer's husband was a very different man, his patience, love and affirmation precious to her. Still, each afternoon as she prepared the evening meal, and each night as she sat down to the table with her family, those fears, firmly rooted in the past, surfaced. Often as Jennifer spooned the potatoes onto her children's plates, her hands would still tremble. Our kitchen table stories will be as unique as we are, some recalled with warm reassurance, some with pain, and others with indifference. Regardless, we have been shaped by them and profoundly so. I once heard the Catholic writer Henri Nouwen describe the table as the 'barometer' of our lives. Sitting together at the kitchen table can be hot or cold, heaven or hell, and sometimes both in the same sitting. Its daily-ness and intimacy make it a place of power, a potent and shaping influence in our lives.

Undergirding our assessment of contemporary life at the table, there lurks a persistent narrative of cultural demise: things aren't what they used to be. According to common wisdom, sitting together at the kitchen table is an endangered act, edging ever closer to extinction. This belief flourishes when the mistiness of our rear view is matched by the jaundiced nature of our perspective on the present. The trouble with misty eyes is they keep us from seeing clearly.

Research certainly confirms that the regular household habit of eating together is challenged, a challenge underlined by significant social change: things like the increasing number of single-person households; the rising participation of both parents in the workforce; the rate of divorce and relationship breakdown; increasing work hours; and the escalating popularity of takeaway food and dining out. There is also evidence that Australian families are cooking less than they once did, finding it harder to balance the demands of work and home, and competing with the distractions of television, computer games and social media. Regardless, research also shows that the concept of eating together retains an important place in the hearts and minds of many Australians, the majority in fact. What's more, we are doing it more commonly than we assume.

The fact is, seventy-eight percent of meals in Australia are still cooked and eaten in the home. What's more, according to the findings of social researcher Rebecca Huntley, more than seventy-five percent of households are frequently eating those meals together at the kitchen table, and when they do, just less than half are staying there for an average time of twenty-five minutes. Perhaps we are not doing quite as badly as we thought. Despite the demands of our working lives and the craziness of our daily schedules, many of us are still working hard to make it happen. Why? Because we believe in it. And we believe in it because we know, intuitively, that the kitchen table is a formative place, one essential to our personal, family and community wellbeing.

In his book *Feast: Why Humans Share Food*, the noted Cambridge archaeologist Martin Jones provides a fascinating exploration of why and how humans eat together. Spanning half a million years of human history, Jones demonstrates just how in-built is our need to sit in community at the table. Certainly the table is a more recent invention and culturally specific in its form, but our habit of gathering around it builds on a universal and deeply rooted human practice of gathering to eat, in its most ancient form around the campfire. Jones calls this the 'conversation circle' and demonstrates the vital role it has played in the biological and social nourishment of humankind. While the nature of our campfire has changed, our need for it has not.

In the final chapter of his book, Jones notes the most recent changes to this campfire: it has been both 'democratised' and 'virtualised'. No longer does the standard image of the family patriarch sitting at the head of the table overseeing his domain, consort to his right, describe reality in the suburban heartlands of Australia. Households of today take multiple forms, and old hierarchies are challenged if not debunked altogether. Further, the conversation circles once defined by our most immediate relationships, eyed across the flames of the campfire, are now radically extended. The technologies of modern life make our tables numerous and, most commonly, they are not the sort we can put our feet under. We are bound across cities, nations and the globe by networks, ideas, interests and partnerships that have little to do with physical act of sharing food.

With Jones, I can rejoice in this more democratic and inclusive household table. I am not one of those who pines for old-fashioned family values or argues for the supremacy of a particular version of family life. And with Jones, I can celebrate the new virtual forms of community now open to us. My household is as wired as any other; smart phones, tablets and laptops are gifts we embrace. No doubt, these new campfires are dazzling, fraught with new challenges but full of possibility. Where Jones and I differ, though, is in what of the old campfire we are prepared to relinquish as we grasp for the new.

The most tangible and daily campfire at the heart of my home remains a table, a real table made of Tasmanian ash by a family friend. It is a beautiful piece of furniture, obviously worn from years of daily use, but still beautiful. In our most recent move, the tabletop was dropped and split in two. Sitting at the centre of our living room, the top, now reattached, sustains a clean break down its middle, obvious to anyone who looks closely. One day we'll have it fixed, but for now it doesn't matter. Like each of us who gather around it, our table is broken but holding together well enough.

Eating Heaven

As I have done for the last twenty years or so, mustering whatever patriarchal authority my family still allows me, I will continue to insist that we sit together at this table as often as life allows. I will keep preparing real food, setting the table with real cutlery and glassware, lighting a real candle and reaching out to hold whatever hands there are with me as we share gratitude for what's in front of us. I will continue to prioritise the practice of being together around the table, eye to eye, insisting that the television is off and the phones with their instant messages and Facebook alerts are set aside, choosing this conversation circle over others for however many minutes we have to share. I will keep doing so because I believe it matters.

Granted, it's a challenge, a daily challenge. My partner and I both work full-time outside the home. My children are teenagers with exhausting social lives and part-time work schedules of their own. There have been times when my insistence on the table has met with biting disapproval: 'Why can't we be normal like everyone else?' Times when our practice of holding hands and saying grace has caused embarrassment in front of friends. Times when my flickering candle was near extinguished by heated words spat across the table. And times when the unavoidable realities of our lives have seen the table sit empty. But we have persisted. Why? Because, along with many other households just like ours and different, we believe this campfire is important. This kitchen table with a crack down its centre holds a formational power unequalled by others; sacred in the richest sense of the word.

◆ RECIPE

Mum's Chocolate Pudding

If you're after a decadent chocolate torte or rich, complex mousse using single origin chocolate from Ecuador, this one will disappoint. As a mid-week family dessert, it's as simple as they come, using nothing but a heaped spoonful of sifted cocoa. With the sound of my chocolate purist friends weeping in the corner, I've toyed with the idea of sprucing it up, adding a little finesse here and there, but it's Mum's recipe and if I mess around with it too much it's no longer hers. Besides, it's good ... plate-licking good! Why mess with a good thing?

Ingredients
- 3½ cups of milk
- 3 heaped tablespoons of cornflour
- 3 tablespoons of sugar
- 1 heaped tablespoon of sifted cocoa
- 1 teaspoon of vanilla essence

Method
- Combine the cornflour, sugar and cocoa together with half a cup of milk, stirring to a thin paste and ensuring there are no lumps. Set aside.
- In a heavy-based saucepan, bring the remaining three cups of milk, with vanilla added, to a boil on a very low heat, stirring routinely so the milk doesn't catch on the bottom.
- Take the boiling milk off the heat and pour in the chocolate paste, stirring vigorously. The mixture should thicken immediately.
- Return the saucepan to the low heat and bring the mixture back to the boil, stirring constantly.
- Divide the mixture between six small dessert bowls and place them in the refrigerator to set.

- When you're ready, serve the bowls as they are with a plastic bottle of cream on the table and a generous supply of sugar close by. No looks of disapproval allowed!

* Ok, so I can't help myself. Once the mixture is ready to pour it into the dessert bowls, I have been known to add a few generous squares of good-quality, dark and bittersweet chocolate, stirring them in until they melt. But don't tell Mum!

CHAPTER 3

The Backyard Table
Eating, Sustainability and Suburbia

Backyards are not what they used to be. Or so they say. Apparently the chook sheds and backyard dunnies of yesterday have given way to swathes of varnished decking, six-burner barbecues and infinity-edged lap pools. But someone forgot to tell Clare.

I meet Clare one clear spring morning in her backyard in Footscray. Once described by a pompous, eastern suburbs newspaper columnist as Melbourne's 'suburban armpit' – probably one who had never actually been there – Footscray is the unofficial capital of the city's inner west, traditionally the lungs of Melbourne industry with the odours of the Altona smelters wafting across its flat landscape. It's also the spiritual home to the beloved Doggies – the AFL's Western Bulldogs. More devout and one-eyed followers you'll never meet.

Armpit no longer, today you need a small fortune to buy in Footscray. Proximity to the city is everything, and on that front, this suburb scores. Just ten minutes on the train and you're in the heart of Melbourne's CBD. What's more, what used to be the working-class inner west has gathered cred as a multicultural cornucopia, mixing young professionals from the east on a mission to gentrify with the persistent waves of immigration, traditionally from places like Italy and Yugoslavia and today from Vietnam and East Africa. This part of town is now 'cool' in an understated, western suburbs kind of way. The cafés are numerous and the plethora of eating houses extraordinary. But walk the streets from the train station to Clare's house and you are in no doubt this is no leafy east. No matter how much has changed, house after house, this is still very much home to working Melbourne. It's still the west, after all.

Clare is quietly spoken, in her mid-thirties, originally from Townsville in north Queensland; an economist by training. We met through mutual friends after I read something Clare had written on the nurturing of the 'households arts'. I was intrigued. After meeting at Clare's front door and wandering our way through to the back, we sit together under the Hills Hoist clothes line that stands with a characteristic lean in the middle of the yard. A few odd socks, a pair of undies and a child's T-shirt hang on its edge. There's no decking in sight, but there is a tin shed behind us attached to a dilapidated cubby house, and a chook shed in the opposite corner. The feathered inhabitants are scratching about in the dirt and making chook-appropriate noises.

In the tree that overhangs the chickens is a makeshift treehouse for Clare's two daughters. Her partner David made it just a few months back and it's been a big hit. 'They outgrew the cubby house!' Clare says with a smile. Most of the backyard is taken up with what looks like ad-hoc veggie patches, overgrown. But when I ask Clare to walk me round and tell me what's there, I soon realise my 'ad hoc' and 'overgrown' does Clare and her yard a serious injustice. This is an intentional place and Clare's passion for it is clear.

'We can start over here.' Clare stands and leads me to the back door, just a few steps from where we are sitting. She points down at the beginning of the garden bed that runs along the back wall of the house: 'Just here we've got spinach, then the broad beans, and along here we'll plant tomatoes in the next month or so.' Clare had already told me she's a keen bottler and works with friends to bottle a year's supply of tomatoes every season for her family and others. 'What we grow ourselves is probably only a few months' worth so we buy boxes of tomatoes at the market and bottle those too. It's great fun. There are people and tomatoes everywhere!'

'You bottle other things too?' I had spied more than tomatoes in the glass jars lining the shelves in Clare's kitchen.

'Yeah, we do lemons, apricots, peaches. There's a peach tree down this way.' Clare points vaguely over her side fence. 'We did cherries one year. We've done figs, apples, pears, plums.'

'You buy them all at the market?' I ask, wide-eyed.

'No, it's mainly stuff we source from the neighbourhood.'

I look perplexed.

'Yeah, there's fruit trees all over the place around here. I remember when I first moved in I noticed Carol around the corner had this apricot tree with the apricots just rotting on the ground, and I thought that is just wrong. So now I just go and knock on people's doors and say 'G'day, I live just down the street. I notice your tree has lots of fruit. Can I have some?' And the response is always "Yeah, go for it! Do you need a bag? Can I get you a ladder?"' Clare looks down, pushing something around the dirt with the edge of her sandal. 'One day Edie, a friend of mine, came with me to do this big neighbourhood grazing trip.' She looks up at me with a grin. 'We had three kids between us, and we put a load of boxes in the back of the station wagon and went to about ten houses in a couple of hours. Mainly lemons. The harvest was amazing!'

We get back to the tour.

'This here is the broccoli.' Clare pulls up some netting from the dirt surrounding it. 'It's only half alive! This was our lame attempt to keep the birds off but it didn't work, so there's only one broccoli left.' There's no disappointment in Clare's voice, just the laid-back resignation of a seasoned gardener. Failure is as standard as success when it comes to growing food. Or so I'm told. 'Here's our year's supply of garlic.' Clare's energy increases. 'We just did one bed this year. Last year we did two and gave a lot away. It's so easy to grow!'

From there we move to the raised beds purpose-built along the side fence. 'Potatoes in here,' Clare says, pointing at the dirt. I nod, mystified. 'They're just starting to come up. And a few little carrots in there. These are more broad beans, and then the snow peas.' Clare winces. 'They would have been wonderful climbing up here, but they keep getting eaten. I just can't make it work.' Personally, this apparent victory of broad beans over snow peas feels like a serious injustice. Frankly, snow peas are divine and broad beans less than palatable no matter what you do to them. I feel Clare's disappointment, but obviously more deeply than she does. She moves on.

'The rocket does its own thing. I love rocket. It just appears! These are onions, and these are runaway raspberries that shouldn't be there. It's not hard to know why they're called a weed. They crop up everywhere.' Clare bends down to pick up a plastic toy that's been dropped beside the wooden sleeper that borders the dirt. 'That's called a tick bean. I must have had them in for about four months,' she says, pointing, resuming the commentary. 'I don't think there's anything in back there.' Clare is nodding her head at a bare patch taken over by something that creeps, 'and we've got some more potatoes over here now.'

We come to a stop by the chook pen. Clare looks wistfully through the wire fence and says nothing. 'You like chooks?' I ask.

'Yeah, I do.' Another long pause. 'We have four chooks now, and the brown one is the old girl. She's been laying. The other three we only got in January and they have just started laying the last month. We are getting about three eggs each day now, so I'll do one egg meal each week. It's great!'

As we move back behind the clothes line, Clare sighs at more raspberries coming up by the compost bins. 'We've got the fruit trees over here, lemons and limes both in pots, and then the arrowroot which has survived the winter, and that's pineapple sage.' We're back to where we began, and Clare retakes her seat.

The only clear ground in the yard is the space we sit on, uneven, directly under the clothes line. This is the spot where Clare and her family sit in their camping chairs to eat dinner when the weather permits. There's no decking in sight, no fancy outdoor table or terracotta pots filled with manicured green to 'balance the room'. It's just this slightly erratic, messy sort of place, but incredibly practical. It's lived in and well loved. As I sit down too, I look back toward the house and notice how well it matches. It's 1950s weatherboard with a back porch walled in to make an extra room. It feels like the flow from the backyard into the house is almost seamless. There's no pretence. It's just home.

The Backyard Table

No doubt, the suburban backyard in Australia has changed along with everything else. Nothing stays the same. Urban historians commonly note the change in our backyards by way of contrast. First there's the difference between the pre-Second-World-War backyard of no-frills utility and production (think veggie garden, lemon tree, chook pen, washhouse and outdoor dunny) and the contemporary preference for recreation, display and the most conspicuous consumption (decking, landscaped garden, swimming pool and Italian sun umbrellas). It was not an overnight change, they say, but a gradual one that has radically altered the nation's backyard landscape.

Second, there's the contrast of intent. 1950s suburbia drew a solid line between the front yard and the back – one commonly as expansive as the other – the front garden a public display of order, decency and good citizenship, and the backyard a hidden and private domain of practicality. Gradually, though, the front yard has shrunk and the back has morphed into an 'outdoor room', an extension of the home's interior design. The backyard is now as important to the public display of 'status' as the front garden ever was. Visit a new display home in the city's thriving outer suburbs, and you can choose your backyard 'style': Australian native, tropical, cottage, Japanese, perfumed, Mediterranean or contemporary.

Third, there's the contrast of economics. It's commonly argued that the pre-war household gave backyard priority to food production because it had no choice. Life in middle Australia, or struggle town as it's been called, with its modest wages and penchant for depression-era thrift, made the backyard part and parcel of the family's survival. Post-Second-World-War, however, life was different. Suburban Australia discovered a level of prosperity unequalled in its brief history. What was once necessity became entirely optional. Out came the veggie gardens and in went the swimming pools.

Certainly, these contrasts contain truth. The backyard has changed, undoubtedly, but sitting with Clare reminds me that the simple dichotomies of history never tell the full story. The truth is, while the broad brushstrokes of time paint changes in our cultural expectations of the backyard, across the suburban heartlands of this country the backyard table retains its links with the soil and with the most immediate expressions of food production and the life that flows from it. It always has.

Growing up in the industrial suburb of 1960s Dandenong – perhaps the city's other 'armpit' – I remember the extraordinary gardens of our Italian neighbours. It wasn't just their backyards that were given over to thriving, compact vegetable kingdoms, but their front yards as well; in fact, any bare piece of earth – front, back or side – was claimed for planting. It's a familiar theme in our story of immigration often missed in the 'broad brushstrokes' approach to backyard history, the one where the Anglo-Australian story supercedes all others. The truth is, in the successive waves of immigration to the suburbs, it's been in the backyard where these new arrivals have staked their cultural claim, and still do, planting in ways that look back to what they've left behind and forward to a new beginning. In fact, it has been so from the earliest days of white settlement. Historians Holmes, Martin and Mirmohamadi illustrate this beautifully in their book *Reading the Garden*, documenting the powerful role the garden has played in our assimilation into this new and strange land:

> The longer colonists stayed here, planting their gardens and creating communities around them, the greater the sense of connection. The memories the garden carried became not only one of 'home', but of their new life in this new place.

The backyard table has always had an immediate connection to the soil around it, and my sense is it always will. In her book *Harvest of the Suburbs*, Andrea Gaynor estimates that every second or third suburban household still provides some of its own food. In a sense, less has changed than we might have imagined. Commentators talk about a twenty-first century renaissance of backyard food production, but perhaps the renaissance is really more in our desire to talk and write about it than in our practice. Similar peaks of interest were noted in the 1970s and again in the late 1980s. It's true, talk about sustainability in energy consumption and local food production is currently riding a wave of popularity, something worth celebrating, but perhaps the backyard gardener has been toiling away all this time with little recognition or cultural fanfare. Take a stroll through the backstreets of your neighbourhood and you'll no doubt see the overhanging lemon trees, the passionfruit vines trailing garage sidings, the herb gardens, and, at the right time of year, the tomato plants being nurtured into fruit. It's there, a great suburban tradition, and Clare is part of it.

As we cradle our mugs of tea, Clare explains where her interest in gardening started. She and David moved down to Melbourne originally to be a part of an intentional community in the heart of the city, one responding to the needs of the city's poor and marginalised – the homeless, drug addicted and mentally ill. They share a deep Christian faith and felt that if their faith didn't translate into a different way of living, then it really had no substance, so here was a good opportunity to see if faith had legs. Once they arrived and immersed themselves in their new work, Clare's interest in gardening began.

'We lived on the eighth floor of a city building,' Clare explains, 'and we had a wooden fire escape by our back door with plenty of sun. I guess there was something about living in the midst of all this concrete that brought out a need to have things alive and growing. I just started with a few polystyrene boxes with cherry tomatoes and rosemary.' 'It's that rosemary there,' Clare says pointing to the small bush by the back door, 'so it's kicked on!' She pauses with a sense of satisfaction, then continues: 'When our time in the city came to an end, and we moved out here, I thought what a great opportunity. I can do more than a few pots on a fire escape, and it's kinda grown since then.'

As the sun re-emerges from behind a solitary thin cloud, I feel its warmth on my forehead. As I look up I see a spider's web in one corner of the Hills Hoist, illuminated by the sunlight. I adjust my chair slightly to avoid squinting. Comfortable again, I ask Clare what role her religious faith plays now she and her family are out here in Footscray. She hesitates, and stares into the distance for a long moment. The words come slowly, but they do come.

Clare talks about the formative influence of writer Wendell Berry. Berry's deeply spiritual and stridently political commentary on issues of land and agriculture has found an audience far beyond the borders of his homeland in rural Kentucky. 'Berry talks a lot about brokenness,' Clare says, 'and our role in human life to restore what is broken. I've always seen that really clearly in terms of people and that was a huge part of what we did in the city. But I now see that role, that vocation of life, much more broadly, of restoring the earth, the land. I feel now that's deeply connected to who we are and what we are made for.' Again there is a long pause. 'The creation stories in Genesis have always been important to me. I feel like I'm much clearer now that we are actually made for the earth, to be sustained by the earth, I mean physically sustained and not just some kind of out-of-body, spiritual thing. It's meant to be earthed. You've got to get your hands dirty.'

Clare is no evangelist. The words and thoughts come slowly, carefully. There's no sense I'm being sold something here, but as Clare talks the garden around her makes more and more sense. I've heard Clare and David talk publically about a concept they call household economy. Clare's first professional appointment as a young economist was in Canberra. Though she went to the national capital with a great sense of vision to be part of social change, to make a difference, the disillusionment was stark. 'It was all so disconnected, so aloof,' Clare says, waving a persistent fly from the rim of her mug. 'I worked on issues to do with child support, really hard and contentious issues. There's a lot of anger when it comes to children and money. But here I was sitting in a glass office, writing papers and making rules about people I knew nothing about. I felt like I was so far removed. I just couldn't get past it.'

Still an idealist, still committed to making change happen, Clare's focus shifted. Rather than working for change from the top down, or from Canberra out, her own efforts for change had to be earthed in the local and with real people. It's this change in focus that brought her and David to Melbourne, and the same commitment that permeates their presence in Footscray. 'I guess what I've come to learn is that the home and what happens in the home, the neighbourhood and what happens in this street, and all the smallest commitments to living generously and in ways that are restorative – all of that permeates the rest of life.'

'So restoration begins here,' I prod, 'from this grand narrative of change to your own backyard?'

'Yeah, that's right,' Clare responds, 'so what you choose to do with food or with time, what you choose to do with income or friendships, the priorities that you set and live by in the smallest ways … it's all this that makes a difference.'

It's a common theme in the grassroots sustainability movement: change begins in our own backyards. Granted, it's not always shaped by explicitly religious convictions as it is for Clare; perhaps not often at all. But there is a common spirituality that undergirds it, a sense of the connection between things, an ecology of complex interdependence that permeates the conversations people are having and the choices communities are making for more sustainable ways of living the 'Australian Dream'.

My beloved brought home a cookbook not long ago – always an act of hope for one who rarely cooks – a gathering of recipes called *The Sustainable Table*. Published by a small non-profit by the same name, it's a gathering of stories and recipes from a whole swag of people passionate about food and committed to more sustainable ways of producing, preparing and sharing it – from people who work in the local food service sector to backyard gardeners like Clare. Together they celebrate this ecology of interdependence and are, in their own small ways, working to help overcome the environmental challenges of today's world table 'one meal at a time'. The book itself, like so many others on today's culinary bookshelves, is an encouragement to home cooks to cook seasonally, shop locally, buy ethically, reduce food waste and make our backyards productive once more. It is these commitments that people like Clare and David are living each day.

The one thing Clare hasn't mentioned in the grand garden tour is the wobbly barbecue that's propped up by the potted fruit trees. I noticed it when I first walked in the yard, which probably says more about me than the barbecue. When I ask about it, Clare smiles. 'It looks a bit dodgy, doesn't it? We haven't used it since last summer so it's a bit neglected.' Clare assures me that come the warmer months the barbecue gets an almost constant workout: 'Yeah, it's pull up a chair, put out a rug; friends, family, neighbours, whoever.'

'What do you cook?'

'Oh, all sorts of things really,' she says, 'depending on who's coming. Lots of sausages, the girls like those, lamb chops are always good, and then heaps of veggies from the garden. We grill zucchinis. We get loads of eggplant in our food co-op box so lots of those go on too. Potatoes, onions, and then all the salad stuff: tomatoes and lettuce. Capsicums too, though ours are a bit slow. We're often not eating them until April, but they come in the box too, so yeah, plenty of those. And then whatever everyone else brings really. It's good fun.'

It's true that in our evolving relationship with the backyard, not everyone feels the same commitment to the garden as Clare does. Dirt under the nails is not everyone's first love. Perhaps a bit of landscaping appeals, with a couple of terracotta pots thrown in. Regardless, what generally unites the backyards of Australia, decked or not, is the presence of the barbecue. Even on my inner-city balcony, there it sits in all its mundane glory.

Food historian Barbara Santich describes the barbecue as the quintessential 'emblem of Australian hospitality'. We own it with a passion. In truth, we didn't invent the barbecue, either as a way of cooking – that came from the Caribbean – or as an event. We imported the backyard version of the barbecue from California, and not until after the Second World War. But we've adopted it with such enthusiasm that we've made it our own in quite distinctive ways. So much so, it's now hard to imagine the backyard table in Australia without it.

New settlers in this country acclimatised to the idea of outdoor dining early on. Our passion for heading out into the bush with food supplies was well in place by the mid 1800s. The introduction of the grilled chop, cooked over an open fire, made a form of picnic that was uniquely

Australian and wonderfully egalitarian. Everyone could do it! In fact, this precursor to the Aussie barbecue was commonly called the 'chop picnic', a term still used well into the 1950s. So popular was this bush picnic that the annual holidays of Christmas, Boxing Day, New Year's Day, Easter and the royal birthdays became excuses for picnicking on an extraordinary scale. The railways of the major cities set up special services to meet the demand.

Infatuated post-war with all things American, and propelled by our rush to detached housing in the burgeoning suburbs, Australians embraced the new Californian fashion of the wood-fired, purpose-built barbecue in the backyard. By the late 1940s, *Home Beautiful* was supplying detailed plans for the home handyman and barbecues were built at extraordinary speed. As Santich says, 'the old chop picnic was taken over and taken home.' The barbecue's domestication was complete. This new form of domesticated bush cooking was a hand-in-glove fit for Australia's flourishing suburban culture: outdoors, wonderfully informal, egalitarian and free from convention. Traditional dining room hierarchies and etiquette could be left indoors where they belonged. This was communal and BYO. What more could you want?

There is an abundance of words written on the deeper meanings of our barbecue culture, an entertaining fruit salad of insight and cliché, some of it helpful. Sociologists Fiske, Hodge and Turner in their book *Myths of Oz* describe the backyard barbecue as the 'high altar' in our Australian rituals of outdoor living. It's secret, they argue, is in the barbecue's ability to keep it all as close to nature as possible. 'The ritual of the barbecue is as formal and culture-created as a high church mass,' they say, 'yet its appeal is its apparent informality and naturalness.'

In their argument, this trio draws on the work of the influential twentieth-century French anthropologist Claude Levi-Strauss. His contention is that nature becomes culture through the processes of cooking. Raw food is raw nature and can't be accepted into culture without the transformative process of the kitchen. While animals eat raw meat, humans eat cooked meat. At the high end of culinary culture, the dinner party is perhaps the most elaborate expression of culture with its place settings, crystal butter dishes and fancy candelabra. Second rung is the family meal, one subject to fewer cultural processes and expectations. Sauce bottles on the table are acceptable. At the lowest end is the outdoor barbecue, where the food and utensils are as close to natural as possible and etiquette and cultural embellishments are kept to a minimum. As an expression of our distinctively informal approach to relationships and our natural connection to the landscape, this ritual of the barbecue is said to suit us well. Apparently those archetypal images of the itinerant bushman or the swagman brewing tea over the campfire still resonate:

> The outdoors of the suburban home acts as a compressed signifier for this image of Australian existence, renovating our irrevocable urbanism by overlaying it with a sense of harmony with nature, of being at ease in, and preferring, the outdoor environment to the constraints of the home.

So, suburbanites, relax and have another sausage!

To be honest, it doesn't do it for me, not entirely. I've never brewed tea on a campfire, and when I look at what shows up at a barbecue these days, the effort required gives dinner party preparation a good run for its money. Still, the informality remains. The barbecue is a different way of being together, and the menu is certainly more ad hoc or 'pot luck', as the Americans say. Invite the neighbours into the dining room for a sit-down three-course dinner, and the invitation is laden with conventions and anxieties. But invite them into the backyard, asking them to bring the coleslaw and beer, and the whole experience is different.

Other commentators say that our infatuation with the barbecue is closely tied to the 'masculinity' of the ritual and the related addiction to meat, the bloodier the better. Alan Saunders takes it back to the English preference for roast beef over the more complex preparations of the French. Quoting an eighteenth-century champion of the English roast and its inherent virility: 'consume roast beef, the mighty roast beef, and your blood will be enriched; you will imbibe the bull-like qualities of nobility and courage. Ragouts, on the other hand, will render you womanish.' Certainly the early settlers in Australia came with a love of meat that only deepened with the years. The historian Geoffrey Blainey, in his delightful *Black Kettle and Full Moon*, reflects on the extent of this meat addiction:

> Some history books suggest that visitors a century ago were surprised the most by Australia's radical politics, particularly the secret ballot and the vote for most men. Visitors, however, were surprised less by the vote than by the meat. That every man could vote was interesting. That nearly every man and woman could eat meat at every meal was astonishing.

In 1890, the average Australian was eating a third of a kilo of meat each day, more than twice that of the average Englishman or American, four times as much as the Germans and the French, and twelve times the allowance of the Italians. According to Blainey, 'to know the full taste of meat was to be an Australian.' While the discrepancies today are not nearly so marked, we are still known as among the most ravenous meat eaters on the planet. The food journalist David Dale makes a connection common to popular commentary on the barbecue between our modern infatuation with meat and the ancient role of men as the tribal hunters:

> Males, who had evolved as hunters of the woolly mammoth, needed to reassert their traditional role as 20th-century civilization closed in on them. They may not have actually killed the meat, but they were able to gain primal satisfaction from heaving bleeding slabs of it on to a metal rectangle they'd souvenired from atop a manhole. The women of the tribe, meanwhile, stayed inside the cave putting salads and crisps into tupperware bowls.

Again, while it all makes for a good barbecue story – and perhaps there are still those men for whom grilling at the hotplate makes them feel more masculine – the cliché of the repressed hunter or master bushman lurking in every suburban bloke clutching his barbecue tongs is all a bit tired and out of cultural steam; as is the image of the apronned woman with children at her feet and her hands in the coleslaw. These predictable clichés are as familiar as they are culturally exclusive and, not surprisingly, most often penned by men. Barbara Santich suggests that the post-war relegation of the man outdoors to the virtually foolproof task of cooking the meat was more likely to do with the woman's ability to get him out of the kitchen while she took charge of the more complex tasks indoors.

The suburbs of today have changed, just like our backyards. Gender roles are in flux, as are the patterns of family life and relationships. The cultural and religious diversity of our neighbourhoods is more notable every day. My own feeling is that we end up diminishing the cultural insight we can take from the still-ascendant barbecue if we surrender to such narrow and reductionist readings of it. Surely the lasting secret of the barbecue is in its adaptability, its flexibility, its capacity as a cultural ritual to enfold and include multiple experiences, stories and cuisines as they arrive.

Greek-Australian writer Christos Tsiolkas' much acclaimed novel *The Slap* was the local publishing sensation of 2008. It's a gruelling story set in suburban Melbourne that was made into an equally gruelling miniseries for ABC television. It's not easy reading. The story begins, however, with a backyard barbecue to celebrate Hector's fortieth birthday. As a gathering of friends and family, there is so much about the picture that Tsiolkas paints that feels like you've been there before. In fact, as confronting as the characters in this story are, perhaps its success is partly in that sense that you already know them. Regardless, it's a telling backyard vignette that illustrates the more likely reality of today's barbecue fare:

> It was a feast. Charred lamb chops and juicy fillet steak. There was a stew of eggplant and tomato, drizzled with lumps of creamy melted feta. There was black bean dahl and oven-baked spinach pilaf. There was coleslaw and a bowl of Greek salad with plump cherry tomatoes and thick slices of feta; a potato and coriander salad and a bowl of juicy king prawns. Hector has been completely unaware of the industry in the kitchen. His mother has brought pasticcio, Aisha had made a lamb in a thick cardamom-infused curry, and together they had prepared two roast chickens and lemon-scented roast potatoes. There was tzatziki and onion chutney; there was pink fragrant taramousalata and a platter of grilled red capsicum, the skins delicately removed, swimming in olive oil and balsamic vinegar.

> The guests lined up for plates and cutlery and the children ate seated around the coffee table. There was hardly any conversation: everyone was too busy eating and drinking, occasionally stopping to praise his wife and his mother for the food.

Now there's a feast! As Santich says, at its best, the backyard barbecue 'spreads its arms and welcomes all' to its multicultural table. Put a backyard and a barbecue together and you've got something potentially magic amidst today's suburban diversity: a relaxed intimacy mixed with an open and welcoming informality. Depending on one's view of the suburban form, the barbecue could be understood as the gift suburbia has bestowed upon us or as a means to its salvation. The writer Marion Halligan claims it as the former, extolling suburbia as one of the great achievements of the human spirit:

> In one's own place, with one's own space, that one creates and cultivates, that one cossets and cares for, with shelter and privacy and comfort, where one can eat and sleep and live and work, invite one's friends, sit under one's own cucumber vine, that site of homely bliss, there is wine and olives and oil and pomegranates, grain and honey and milk, even if most of these have come from the supermarket. The perfect life ...

A more cynical view, dismissive of Halligan's notion of the 'promised land' through the back door, wants to hold suburbia with its hidden backyards to account as a sort of 'privatopia' that cossets people securely in residential isolation. Either way, as gift or salvation, the barbecue wins. In poll after poll, Australians rate common barbecue fare as close to a national dish as we have. There's something about the backyard barbecue that continues to resonate as an appropriate national symbol, a relaxed ritual of welcome and inclusion that says something about who we are.

In an ever more paranoid age of cultural suspicion and border protection, when we're pressured to lock the gates and draw the curtains, there's something to be said for reclaiming the backyard and its barbecue as more than just a quirk of Aussie culture. Perhaps how we live in our backyards, what we invest in our backyard tables, what's on our plates and whom we invite to join us, can be powerful statements about the sort of society we aspire to and the communities we want to be part of. I reckon Clare is right: 'what you choose to do with food or with time, what you choose to do with income or friendships, the priorities that you set and live by in the smallest ways ... it's all this that makes a difference.'

◆ RECIPE

Vietnamese Coleslaw

What's a suburban barbecue without the 'slaw? It's just not. Coleslaw and potato salad, along with the sausages, bread and sauce: it's all we ever needed. In backyards from Freemantle to Coburg, generations of apron-wearing Anglo-Aussies have piled the wooden salad bowl full of the stuff, each household with its variation on the standard mix of shredded cabbage, grated carrot, salad onion and, if you're keen, a handful of sliced celery. Mix it together with a good blob of mayonnaise, a few spoonfuls of sour cream, and a little oil, vinegar and sugar. My mum added apple, which I always thought to be an exotic departure from the norm. I liked it.

Things have changed. Today's backyard menu is barely recognisable from the past, but the coleslaw remains. As our smoky gatherings have embraced the food traditions of other places, so the old 'slaw has found new life. Frankly, it's vastly improved. Let's be honest, the Vietnamese outdo us in the salad department hands-down, and coleslaw is no exception. Here's a recipe adapted from *The Sustainable Table* that in turn pays tribute to Australian chef Stephanie Alexander. My family loves it!

Ingredients

Dressing

- 3 cloves of garlic, finely chopped
- 1 long red chili, finely sliced. If you like the heat, keep the seeds intact. If not, scrape them out.
- ⅓ cup of fresh lime juice
- A splash of rice vinegar
- ⅓ cup of fish sauce
- ¼ cup of sugar

Salad
- ½ Chinese cabbage, finely shredded
- 1 carrot, peeled and coarsely grated
- 1 daikon, peeled and grated
- 1 red onion, finely diced
- ½ cup of fresh coriander leaves
- 1 cup of fresh mint leaves
- ½ cup of fried noodles
- 1 tablespoon of dried fried onions

Method
- To prepare the dressing, combine all the ingredients, mix well, cover and set aside.
- In a large bowl combine the cabbage, carrot, daikon and red onion.
- Set aside a few coriander and mint leaves for decoration, then roughly chop the remainder and add to the cabbage mix.
- Add the dressing to the salad mix and toss the whole thing together.
- Just before you need it, arrange the salad on a platter and scatter over the fried noodles and onions.
- Finally, decorate the salad with the few remaining coriander and mint leaves.
- Eat! It's really good, especially with those chili seeds left in.

CHAPTER 4

The Café Table
Eating, Sidewalks and Community

Hardware Lane stretches discreetly between Bourke and Little Lonsdale Streets and just a few minutes walk from Melbourne's GPO. It's a narrow little thoroughfare, a mixture of cobblestones and asphalt; one of many just like it that crisscross the city's central district. These lanes are a vital component of Melbourne's Hoddle grid – the mathematically aligned matrix of streets that distinguishes this city's urban form.

In 1837 Robert Hoddle was nothing more than an assistant to the colony's Surveyor General – and one thought to be only moderately gifted – when charged with bringing order to the development of this southern outpost. His boss had prior commitments to a book tour in England. It turns out that Governor Bourke was suspicious of this new Port Philip settlement, a young upstart in the colony, and wanted to ensure it was brought to heal and order. What better way than to impose over it a regimented street form, 'an assertion of civilization against wildness' as historian Andrew Brown-May describes it. Hoddle's first draft did not include laneways like this one. It was the good governor who demanded the insertion of 'little streets' to provide rear access and mews for the substantial allotments on the major boulevards. In no time at all the city's rapid growth and associated commercial interests saw these backyard thoroughfares take on a life of their own.

Today's Hardware Lane is lined with cafés and restaurants interspersed with spas, hairdressers, a camera store, a drycleaner and locksmith, a real estate agent, travel agent and ski shop. But mainly it's a place to eat; a place to sit, linger with a café latte and watch life wander by. For this purpose, every establishment has outdoor seating. In other places it's called footpath or sidewalk seating, but here the term is superfluous. Given the bulk of the lane is closed to traffic for most of the day, Hardware is nothing but sidewalk.*

The central stretch of the lane was originally home to Kirk's Horse Bazaar, a busy horse- and livery-trading centre from the 1840s. In many cases, the veneers of the original warehouses and stables are still intact, the central ones designed by William Pitt, the celebrated architect responsible for some of the city's finest Gothic Revival buildings. While the remaining warehouses don't have quite the presence of his grand Princess Theatre, there is still beauty to them. Today the horses are gone, long gone, and the warehouses transformed into a popular strip of middling eating houses, most claiming 'Italian' fare and fronted by a stream of spruikers enticing customers with their sideshow bonhomie and two-for-one cocktail deals. Regardless, the street still retains a strong sense of its working past and an even stronger sense of neighbourhood for those who live and work there.

Settebello is my café of choice. It hangs just off the end of the restaurant bazaar, a quiet slice of sanity free of the spruikers and their Cheshire-Cat smiles. It sits comfortably at one of Hardware's corners, the one it shares with Little Bourke. It's a place with large windows and an intimate view of Hardware's tree-lined southern end and the passing traffic of Little Bourke that intersects it. It's a vista of small scale with no distractions from the continuous stream of minutiae passing by outside. The window seating along the café's south-facing parameter provides a quiet but absorbing place to sit with paper or book, or a friend if you have one. I often sit here, though friendless most often. For me the liturgical movement of sight between my reading and the view beyond is rhythmic and restful; solitude is an essential part of the ritual.

---

* Throughout this chapter I have chosen to use the North American terminology of the sidewalk café rather than the alternatives of outdoor seating, alfresco dining or with reference to the more Australian 'footpath'. I do so because it describes more succinctly what I am writing about. For those offended by the infiltration of American terminology, my apologies!

The café itself is small, just large enough for a moderately sized communal table at its centre and a few smaller ones around it. The décor hints at 1970s retro with a wallpaper of black and grey geometrical design that I recall from my suburban childhood. The fare is simple, unfussy but of consistent quality – tapas, pizza, focaccia, pastries and a selection of wines by the glass – and the coffee is good. There are two young men who keep the place humming, one a handsome Japanese fellow with a warm, engaging smile and the other a tall, lanky, red-headed barista with glasses. He looks for all the world like Wally, the elusive, beanie-clad character in red and white stripes hiding in the pages of my children's childhood books. The barista is shy I think, trying hard to find his way between friendly and professional, keen to relate but edging on the side of cool reserve.

Outside on the laneway, Settebello provides the mandatory collection of wobbly tables, folded paper or cardboard wedged under one leg to keep them steady and surrounded by those standard-issue, aluminium-frame chairs typical to corners like this one. I sit there too when the rain has cleared and glimpses of blue sky appear, but here my beloved solitude is less common. There are too many familiar faces in Hardware Lane to be left alone for long. It was my neighbourhood for several years and its characters are many.

One of those is Charlie, or Pasquale in his native Italian. In his mid seventies and long past retirement, Charlie is a barber who has cut hair in Hardware Lane for thirty-seven years. Today he works just a few days each week, coming in from his suburban home and beloved garden in Springvale. Blissfully unconcerned about the number of customers he does or doesn't have, Charlie spends most of his time standing in the laneway smoking his cigarettes, downing his potent little shots of espresso or devouring plates of spaghetti under the awning at Max, the restaurant directly opposite his shop; his complimentary lunch a fair trade, he told me once, for cutting the chef's hair at no charge. When he sees me walking by or sitting alone at my café table, he beams and joins me, arms outstretched with a generous smile.

'How are you Charlie?' I say.

'Ah, not bad for an old man!' he retorts predictably as he pulls out a chair to settle in.

We chat easily, he regaling me with stories of his wife's mock 'contempt' of his character and presence. 'That's why I still come to work,' he says with a grin, as though he's never told me before: 'My wife, she says "When are you leaving, Charlie? I have too much to do".' Though age has wearied his face and the cigarettes have taken their toll on his lungs, it is easy to tell he had been a fine-looking young man with well-defined features and a stature to match. His hair is always in place and his dress impeccable: tailored trousers, stylish shirts and smart Italian shoes. Though he never orders his coffee at Settebello, he will stay for as long as I do, as if this chair was his long before the café existed.

And then there's Henry. More often I see him sitting on a seat outside the McDonalds on Bourke Street, but he's learnt to look for me now on Hardware. Henry is a sad character, a ward of the state since childhood and mentally impaired. Though he's older than I am, he's childlike in demeanour, a sweet and gentle soul. Comfortably addicted to nicotine, Henry is blessed with a warm, round face to match his rotund body. When he sees me, his face breaks into his trademark toothless grin. I stand to hug him and he melts into the embrace, as though this may be the only human touch he has from week to week. The stale and blended smell of alcohol and cigarettes surrounds him. I pull out his seat and ask him if he would like a coffee. 'White with two sugars, please,' he says, as though ready for the invitation.

'And a brownie?' I add, knowing his response before he offers it.

'Oh, yes!'

If I see Henry pass by from my indoor window seat, he will wave and smile but wait, never willing to come inside. I suspect he feels uncomfortable indoors, perhaps because he senses other people's discomfort too. But here on the laneway, open to the air and without confinement, Henry relaxes and looks as at home as everyone else. We chat together about the weather, what he's done the last week, and his weekend visit to see his mum. 'She bought me cigarettes,' he reports each time we meet with an endearing sense of gratitude.

The Café Table

The cafés of Hardware Lane – Settebello and its neighbours – are duplicated all across Melbourne and, indeed, the nation. And their sidewalk tables have become the trademark of a thriving, cosmopolitan urban centre. In the City of Melbourne alone, according to its own *Outdoor Café Guide*, there are now six hundred outdoor café venues with some fifteen thousand sidewalk seats representing an increase of more than one thousand percent since 1990. And the number of cafés, with or without the sidewalk, has blossomed beyond all expectation. According to the latest IBISWorld data, the broader food and beverage sector has been growing at an astonishing seven to eight percent every year for the last decade. Nationwide there are now some six thousand five hundred cafés and coffee shops that represent a combined annual revenue of five billion dollars and employ some eighty-one thousand Australians.

There is no doubt that our love affair with the café, and especially its sidewalk seating, is in full bloom with no sign of wilting. It is odd, given Melbourne's unpredictable climate, that our love of the outdoor table is as passionate as it is. We Melburnians will sit anywhere as long as the coffee is good. We'll prop ourselves on milk crates or tiny backless stools with knees tucked under our chins. We'll sit in grungy laneways covered in graffiti and metres from overflowing, industrial-sized rubbish bins. We'll sit on busy thoroughfares with traffic rushing by, just a Perspex barrier between the gutter and us. And we'll sit come rain or shine. Savvy café proprietors now provide stand-alone gas heaters that burn overhead for our comfort; the thought of going indoors is simply too much.

Coffee and its cafés have long been a passion for Melburnians, but in the last decade the passion has morphed into an obsession. Devotees will scour the pages of the numerous guidebooks, newspaper columns and blogs to determine where the latest caffeine hotspots are and how their favourite haunts are measuring up with the competition. Baristas have taken the mantle of 'priest' in these modern temples, dispensing liquid grace and perfection to those who queue routinely at their altars. As the first officially recognised Slow Food City outside of Europe, Melbourne boasts more cafés per head of population than any other city in the nation. Then again, all Australian cities now trumpet their café and alfresco dining credentials, manipulating the statistics to their advantage. While the real truth is muddy and hard to discern, it is sure to smell of coffee. Café culture is now considered essential to a city's prospects and image.

Somewhere along the way, the café and its sidewalk seating has become one of the most recognisable signs of the good life. So much so, the billboards that line the highways on new suburban estates include images of inner-city cafés and lattes against rural backdrops. Savvy suburban developers include outdoor dining spaces to add to the cachet of their instant residential communities, while the property supplements in our newspapers predict the new real-estate hot spots around the suburbs' emerging café strips. The café table has never been so popular.

The origin of coffee and its cafés dates back to ninth-century Abyssinia. We know it today as Ethiopia. The story is told of a goat herder, amused by the friskiness of his goats who had just devoured the beguiling red cherries of the coffee plant. By the mid-sixteenth century, coffee was being roasted, ground and brewed in the cultural Mecca of Constantinople (modern-day Istanbul). From its beginning, coffee's popularity was closely tied to the establishments in which it was served, for this deep brown liquid has ever been as much a social lubricant as a beverage to satiate a thirst.

A century later, and 'coffee houses' had sprouted all across Europe. In 1652 the Sicilian-born Pasqua Rosee opened London's first coffee venue in a churchyard shed. By the 1660s some two thousand coffee houses were spread all across England, Scotland and Ireland. In fact, so important had the coffee house become to social and political networking that Charles II moved to ban them as 'seminaries of sedition'. In 1686 Café Procope became the first commercial establishment in Paris to serve coffee indoors, and by the mid-1800s Paris had more than three thousand of them. In fact, according to coffee historian Andrew May, the mid-ninteenth century in Paris saw the *salon de café* rival 'the neighbourhood, the street, the inn and the cabaret as the new setting for social intercourse'.

Melbourne's nineteenth-century aspiring urban settlers sought similar venues for social connection, though following England's infatuation with tea, coffee was a more marginal obsession. In fact, it was identified more with the working class than it was in other places. While the gentlemen of 1850s Melbourne were taking their tea in the few and exclusive cafés of the town, coffee was being brewed and served from coffee carts sprouting across Hoddle's grid. These mobile providers of the hot beverage were especially popular beside the town's numerous markets. What's more, they were more commonly nocturnal venues that took up their stations after dark and stayed until sunrise. According to May, they were 'a boon for the night-going public, a flickering island of resort and convenience in a dim sea of danger and fatigue'. In their late-night guise, these stalls operated as 'staging posts and places of repose for the straggler or the late-goer on their tired way home, or as dispensers of tonic at the start of a night's shift'.

Predictably, the night-time coffee cart had it detractors. The restaurant proprietors, predominantly at the top end of Bourke Street and close to the Eastern Market that flourished at the corner of Stephens (now Exhibition Street), were resentful of these 'freeloaders' who paid no rent and attracted the wrong sort of people. Support for their presence, however, came from the gathering momentum of the temperance movement, which affirmed these coffee stalls as providing a constructive alternative to the 'demon drink'. Indeed, the popularity of the town's coffee carts led to the 1880s development of Melbourne's coffee 'taverns', essentially places that provided refreshment and accommodation free of alcohol's dark influence.

These 'coffee palaces' were grand affairs. There was the two-hundred bedroom Melbourne Coffee Palace on Bourke Street, Spring Street's Grand Coffee Palace (now the Windsor Hotel), and the renowned Federal Coffee Palace on the corner of Collins and King, a place that boasted five hundred rooms – drawing rooms, reading rooms, sitting rooms and bedrooms – and the largest dining hall in the country. Ultimately all of

Eating Heaven

these venues failed in the 1890s crash, with some securing liquor licenses to survive. The humble coffee cart, however, continued on the town's street corners into the twentieth century. Eventually, though, as tea made its persistent ascension, coffee fell away as a beverage of choice, even among the working people. By 1910 the coffee carts were all but gone.

Melbourne of the 1920s birthed a handful of indoor coffee lounges, but with the return of servicemen from the First World War, the city saw a spike in the demand for the 'continental style' café. By 1939 there were four hundred and fifty registered cafés in Melbourne and coffee consumption had increased by seventy percent. However, it was in the 1950s with the advent of the ever-so-chic European espresso machine that the café edged its way more permanently into Melbourne's urban landscape. All across the city and into its outlying suburbs, these gleaming contraptions introduced a new, more palatable and exciting caffeine experience to the increasingly diverse population of post-war Melbourne. The advent of outdoor seating, however, was slower to arrive.

It was back in 1909 that the noted English churchman, writer and journalist Frederic C. Spurr was appointed the sixth minister of the Collins Street Baptist Church. His ominous profile still looms in a portrait above my desk. On news of his appointment, *The Argus* proclaimed him 'a man of whom any church or city might be proud'. Indeed, Spurr was more than a preacher of the Christian gospel. He was also a public intellectual of note and a keen observer of culture who wrote voluminously of his new home. During Spurr's tenure at Collins Street, he published a series of articles in the *Christian World* on 'life in the commonwealth', a series that generated 'a great amount of interest among all classes' in Australia and Great Britain and created for him 'a vast correspondence'.

In one essay reflecting on the impressive emergence of Melbourne as a city of amenity to compare with any in Europe, Spurr trumpeted the virtues of introducing outdoor seating to its streets and boulevards, those he judged to be 'wide enough to allow for the open-air café'. 'Situated at such a latitude,' he wrote, 'Melbourne lends itself admirably to boulevard life. A touch of Paris would make of Melbourne the most attractive city in this hemisphere.' He bemoaned, however, Melbourne's more likely infatuation with the urban form of America, driven as it was by its dogged pursuit of financial prosperity over cultural amenity. 'The American hustling spirit is manifest here in everything,' he said, 'religion included.'

Indeed, with the residential evacuation to the suburbs, a trend that took root very early in Melbourne's development, the city centre was surrendered to the drab worlds of commerce and government. Come 5pm, its public servants and workers uniformly evacuated to their private suburban havens, places where strict zoning laws precluded the flourishing of unpredictable and unregulated street life. It was not until 1954, as the espresso machine was transforming the city's relationship to coffee, and some four decades after Spurr's impassioned plea, that outdoor seating finally appeared in Melbourne. It was outside the bohemian Mirka's Café on Exhibition Street. In 1958 the Oriental Hotel, just around the corner on Collin Street's 'Paris end', secured permission from the Melbourne City Council to do likewise for a trial period of three months. The trial was judged a failure by the city's bureaucrats, and in 1960 the Police Traffic Branch teamed up with the city's health inspectors to brand such seating unsafe to the wellbeing of the city. The seating was gone with breathtaking speed. The public reaction was equally swift and the outrage intense. Newspaper commentators publically despaired at the power of mindless 'beancounters' who, by enforcement of their endless by-laws-in-duplicate, could render this city an embarrassing backwater in the modern world. Finally, and without fanfare, the seats were restored. Though today the city's by-laws continue to govern the growth of its sidewalk seating, Melbourne has now embraced the café and its outdoor appendices with vigour.

So much has changed about Melbourne since the advent of its outdoor tables. Journalist Royce Millar notes that even in the early 1980s, the CBD was home to just seven hundred people living in two hundred city flats. Today the same neighbourhood provides housing to more than twenty-three thousand residents. As a lived-in city, the centre of Melbourne has transformed from vacant space to one of the most densely populated neighbourhoods in the state. And now the city's street life is bristling. As one of those twenty-three thousand, I live just two minute's walk from the city's Federation Square. Though the city has been my family's home for many years, our housing choice remains a novel one in the suburban heartlands. One of the most common assessments of our neighbourhood from those outside is that we live in 'café heaven'! Indeed, cafés abound in our area and we are constantly grateful, but this alignment of a café with heaven is an interesting one. What is it about a café that we have come to equate with divine worth? And what does our obsession with the café and its tables, outdoor and in, say about our deeper longings and aspirations?

It's communal. As I write, Australians are living in uncertain financial times. Prior to the Christmas season, retailers are nervous about our reluctance to spend. As the nation's Reserve Bank equivocates again over interest rates, retail sales have dropped more than five percent in twelve months. At the same time our spending at the local café is on the rise. In fact, while retail spending flounders, our spending at the nation's cafés and restaurants has climbed by more than eleven percent. The sociologists are saying it's about community.

In an interview with journalist Rachel Wells, Maureen Harrington of Queensland's Griffith University concludes,

> A lot of people see dining out as a way of connecting with friends and family ... They won't go out and buy a big flat-screen TV or new apparel or bed sheets. They'll make do with what they've got so they can still go out for dinner and feel like they have a life.

At its best the café is a place of social connection. Despite our stampede online to virtual places like Facebook and Google+, there is still nothing like sitting at a table with friends, the real flesh-and-blood sort; those who embrace us when we arrive, laugh with us, smile at our stories and frown at our gaffes. It's a place to share our successes and failures, review our loves and losses, plan seductions and map out business strategies on serviettes. It's a place to hear the gossip or share it with secretive relish. Even without a friend to sit with, the café provides a place of connection, carefully managed. At the café I can leave behind the isolation of home or office and sit for a while on a sidewalk, clutching a mug of hot chocolate or dangling the lips in a cup of sweet chai. The café table is a place to go when life is overwhelming or sad, a legitimate place to waste some time, to hide from the rain or cold or gather courage for the next therapy session. And all of this in a place surrounded by others with whom I have no intimate connection but who, for the duration of my stay, share this time and this place with me. As the writer Valerie Clarke says:

> Today, the café remains a place where awnings, tables and chairs await you; a place where you may arrive feeling blue, and then, for no apparent reason, find the mood magically lifting; maybe an idea comes to mind, a friend approaches, the coffee is served. Or perhaps the sun comes out, a breeze stirs, or a favourite song is played. But one thing is evident: at the café one realizes one is not so alone as previously supposed and that life itself can be grand.

It was the twentieth-century French philosopher Jean-Paul Sartre who described the café as a 'fullness of being'. Throughout its history, Sartre and many others like him have found at the café table something life-giving. Most often it has to do with its provision of space that is both personal and public, secluded yet connected. This communion of the café table is not first about intimacy but connection no less. Very often the communal nature of the café is found in its anonymity amidst life. Like travel on public transport where the shared space of train or tram contrast with the private cocoons of car and home, life in the café is the life we have in common. Travel the streets of Melbourne, especially its many 'high streets' lined with sidewalk cafés, and watch the people coming and going, eating and drinking, laughing, reading or just sitting. There is no more immediate or tangible sign of the city in community. Our shared life is not hidden away inside vast shopping malls or behind the high fences of suburbia. Rather, it's on the street and in full view, open and accessible to anyone who chooses to come.

It's local. On a recent visit to Vietnam, my family and I spent time in Ho Chi Minh City, formerly Saigon, a thriving metropolis of nine million people and the nation's most populous. The life of this city is extraordinary. Like many across Asia, it's a place that never sleeps; the relentless surge of people along its lanes, streets and highways, mostly on motorbikes, is a round-the-clock phenomenon. Amidst all this movement, food stalls and sidewalk cafés fill every street corner and are one of the few places where people are still for any length of time. To the naive foreigner, these little 'fuelling stations' all look the same. Many are nothing more than a collection of milk crates or small plastic chairs gathered around a cooking cart or a simmering stockpot propped up on the sidewalk. However, spend just a few days coming and going from the same location and you begin to understand the unique role each one plays. For as I passed one establishment, the same each night, I noticed familiar faces, the same people talking, trading stories, and keeping an eye on the motorbikes propped up on the footpaths around them. Here in the middle of this turbulent mass of movement and change, the corner café is an anchor point. As insignificant as each one might seem on its own, these little feeding spots combined provide the city with a sense of multiple localities that make it a functional whole. The city only thrives as a dense patchwork of little neighbourhoods.

By its nature, the café is local. While the restaurant is more likely to be a stand-alone destination, the café's success depends on its locality and its convenience to home, to work or as a stopover from one place to another. Perhaps the proliferation of cafés and their sidewalks is a re-emergence of locality as a value in Australian city living; a venue of daily life that meets our longing for more organic expressions of community. Though the chains exist – the Gloria Jeans and Starbucks – the vast majority of our cafés are independently owned and operated. The menus are created and food prepared in-house. The person who serves you is just as likely to have a vested interest in the café's viability. It's quirky, hit and miss, and you have to choose carefully. Unlike the standardised experience of the chains, the sidewalk is much less uniform, much less predictable and secure. But it's alive, it's local and it's what we prefer.

Of course, as a local stopover in everyday life, the café is not alone. Ray Oldenburg in his celebrated book *The Great Good Place*, trumpets the role of similar 'third places' of daily life, those that exist somewhere in between the public (work-related) and private (home-related) spheres. The café sits with the tavern, the pub and the beer garden as a place to which we can retreat from the concerns of work and home and delight momentarily in the pleasures of good company and conversation. According to Oldenberg, when the life of the city is devoid of such places, the quality of its social cohesion suffers, as does the vitality of its democracy.

It's humanising. The French social theorist Michel de Certeau once noted the particular pleasure he has in looking down upon a city from the top of its highest building. From this vantage point one sees the whole, he says, and reads the city as a full text, a complete story with all its chapters laid out in sequence. Yet from above one cannot write the story. There on high one can't participate fully in the city's complex and chaotic narrative; one can only observe.

The truth is, a city is so much more than a series of tall buildings, each one stretching up into its own 'quarter-acre' of space. The city is more than a patchwork of streets on Google maps. Row upon row of monolithic structures and the picturesque skylines they create do not a city make. All of this provides the chessboard upon which real life plays out below. For it is down here, in all the in-between places, that the story of the city is written and lived.

The Canadian-American journalist Jane Jacobs once described this life of the city's streets and in its neighbourhoods as a 'dance' of constant movement and change:

> not a simple-minded precision dance with everyone kicking up at the same time ... but an intricate ballet in which the individual dancers and ensembles all have distinctive parts which miraculously reinforce each other and compose an orderly whole.

It is this dance, this 'ballet of the good city sidewalk', that makes the city a place worth being, a human place.

At its best, the café inhabits the in-betweens of the cityscape. It is both intimate and immediate. It's a place that tames the city for those who dance its streets and write its story. As a place of the in-betweens, the café is one of the stations of urban life that make it human, accessible and inclusive of all those who wander its sidewalks.

It's inclusive ... mostly. My friend Henry who sits with me at Settebello is welcome on the sidewalk. For the cost of a coffee he can sit just as long I can. Perhaps he's right; inside the café his presence is obvious, but here on the city's footpath he can smile his toothless grin and enjoy his white-with-two-sugars just like anyone else. It may or may not be comfortable for those around him. Henry is visibly different from many of the café's more regular customers, and his odour is a little more pungent. But as with public transport, this is public space. Cafés may set up their tables and chairs for commercial purposes. They may even mark their territory with planter boxes and screens, but for the most part the sidewalk remains a public place. The by-laws cannot keep Henry at bay.

That said, public space is always contested space. There are competing uses for the city's footpaths and public squares. By its very presence, the sidewalk café precludes other possibilities. A homeless man sleeping rough is not a good look anywhere near those who sip late-night cocktails. Public demonstrations that hinder access to areas of alfresco dining cause tension between those who want to sell the coffee and those who want to publically question the markets of international trade that bring it to us.

This tension was illustrated powerfully in late 2011 when the Occupy Melbourne movement took up temporary residence in the city square. Redeveloped to include cafés and bars around its perimeter with an abundance of outdoor seating, the city's central gathering place must now balance commercial interests with the rights of its citizens to congregate and demonstrate. Kim Dovey, Professor of Architecture at the University of Melbourne, highlights the tensions present in what he calls this 'tranquilisation' of public space. While the benefits it brings to a city and its neighbourhoods are significant, Dovey reminds us of the historic connection between the nature of public space and the flourishing of democracy: 'Democracy is based in citizenship which is anchored and quite literally embodied in the flows of everyday life and patterns of behaviour in public space.' Urban form cannot generate democracy, Dovey concludes, but it can certainly help to sustain an inclusive and democratic form of city life. The line between the inclusive and the exclusive in public space is fine and easily frayed; no less so at the café table.

A few years back my beloved arrived home with a gift. Looking especially pleased with herself, she placed a large, heavy box on the kitchen bench, beautifully wrapped, and stood back with a broad smile. Understanding my cue, I stepped in, unwrapped it expectantly and lifted from the box a beautiful Italian espresso coffee machine. As I placed it carefully on the bench, running my fingers slowly over its curves, my own smile was immediate. It looked every bit as impressive as the retro La Cimbali I had long admired at Quists on Little Collins. I was both enraptured and perplexed.

Indeed, I was enthralled by this sleek machine sitting regally at the centre of my home. The beauty of good design has always held my gaze, and when applied to a substance of life close to my heart, what more could I want? But I was also perplexed. This sleek machine now sat in the privacy of my own kitchen and there was something not quite right. I couldn't immediately put my finger on it, but the discomfort remained.

For the next two days there it stood, untouched and untried. I stared at the machine every time I walked past, occasionally hovering over it as if to understand it better prior to full commitment. Finally, prodded by a beloved bemused by my hesitation, I engaged. Following closely the instructions in the accompanying manual, I stepped my way methodically through the production of my first coffee. After a badly composed symphony of gurgles, drips and hisses, the end result was poor. Worse than poor, it was atrocious, a tart milky-brown water sitting limply in the cup. I retreated, wounded by my own incompetence and offended by the mystery of a machine impervious to my failure. A week later, the machine went back in its box and was patiently returned to the store.

As I have been reminded by my disbelieving friends many times over, the art of the perfect homebrewed espresso takes time. Indeed, I know that well enough, and were it just a matter of an art form to be mastered, the machine would still be in my kitchen. But my home espresso reserve is about more than the absence of skill. For me, there is something about coffee in its most developed form that is deeply tied to the café. Like jazz at its best, once experienced in the dark and moody ambience of a venue dedicated to its performance and appreciation, there is something lost when listening to its pre-recorded rhythms in the privacy of one's living room. The truth is, good jazz is more than the music. It is an experience, a shared experience. You have to be there. The private jazz of the living room may have its place, but there is something about its nature that is essentially public in an intimate sort of way.

So, too, with coffee. The café is about more than flat whites and long blacks perfectly drawn. Coffee is about relationship, connection, theatre and community. Coffee away from the café table may have its comforting part to play in our daily routines. Sitting up in bed with my beloved with the first coffee of the day is as reassuring as any other routine of life. But there remains something about the nature and purpose of coffee that is intimately public. The café table is more than just a convenient place to drink. It is life.

◆ RECIPE

Double Chocolate and Cranberry Brownies

I have always maintained that the test of a good café, or one of them, is the quality of its chocolate brownies. Though not universal to café fare, they should be. I know ... it's an American import. There is certainly no mention of brownies in my tattered 1970s version of *The Australian Women's Weekly Cookbook*. There are plenty of 'squares', 'slices' and 'biscuits', but not a brownie in sight. Still, I like them and given I share my life with a Texan-Australian, I can easily lift my culinary hat where it's deserved. What's more, let's be honest, there are surely few things better for one's mid-afternoon life than a cup of dark, rich espresso served with a dense square of warm, fudgy, nutty, chocolatey whatever-you-call-it.

I make brownies myself. My kids love them. Trouble is, they don't do nuts, so I am forced to improvise. It's been a slow process of elimination, but I have found cranberries, soaked in orange juice or something stronger, an acceptable addition for my ever-critical offspring. They also provide a good diversion for those more astute palates longing for the crunch of walnuts.

Ingredients

- 125 grams of butter
- 150 grams of dark chocolate
- 2 eggs
- 1 cup of castor sugar
- 1 cup of plain flour
- 2 tablespoons of self-raising flour
- ¾ cup of white chocolate buttons
- ½ cup of dried cranberries
- Orange juice

Method
- Grease a 20cm square (or thereabouts) cake tray and pre-set the oven to 180ºC, a little cooler if using a fan-forced oven.
- Place the cranberries in a small bowl with enough orange juice to cover them, and leave to soak for about twenty minutes.
- Meanwhile, combine the butter and dark chocolate in a small saucepan over a very low heat and melt together, stirring gently. Don't walk away! Keep stirring, and once everything is melted and smooth, set the saucepan aside for the contents to cool.
- Place eggs and castor sugar in a bowl or electric mixer and whisk together until pale and thick.
- By hand, fold in the chocolate and butter mixture followed by the flour (plain and self-raising), the drained cranberries and the white chocolate buttons.
- Spoon the gooey mixture into the pre-greased cake tray and bake for around thirty minutes or until the brownie is firm.
- Allow the brownie to cool a little before cutting it into squares. Place the squares onto a beautiful white pedestal cake stand (just because), douse with a fine mist of icing sugar, and eat immediately ... with coffee!

CHAPTER 5

The Five-star Table
Eating, Beauty and Justice

It had been fourteen years, but as my beloved and I made our way beyond the high rendered wall and up the narrow driveway, this grand old house felt more familiar than strange. Following the line of manicured gardens guiding our way on either side and with the upper balcony looming over us, it was clear little had changed. We certainly had. Fourteen years ago we couldn't afford a night like this. With two small children and a PhD in progress, we had just enough to pay the rent but little more. A generous friend had made the booking for us, giving the restaurant instructions about payment and ensuring we were not bothered with the detail. Fourteen years later we were back, and this time paying our own way.

From the long driveway we took the two tiled stairs to the entrance and stood momentarily before a stately wooden door in burgundy. Framed by coloured insets of stained glass, it was an entrance typical of such Victorian-era mansions, slightly intimidating but welcoming no less. Before I could reach for the brass handle, the door opened as if intuitively. 'Good evening.' A young woman, perfectly groomed, stood smiling warmly just beyond the doorframe, gesturing us in. Standing discreetly to one side, she made generous space as we stepped through the door and into the entrance hall, the ceilings high above us, the lamplight soft and the walls a deep chocolate brown. 'Welcome to Jacques Reymond,' she said, as the door closed silently behind us.

Without argument, Jacques Reymond is one of Australia's finest restaurants. Indeed, it has been so for most of its twenty-five years. In the world of fine dining, one year is a long time, twenty-five extraordinary. The name of the restaurant is the name of its chef, an adventurous and talented Frenchman who arrived on these shores via Sao Paolo, Madrid and Paris back in 1983. After an initial and celebrated stint at Miettas, another of Melbourne's legendary eating-houses, Reymond established his own restaurant in Richmond using his wonderfully Gallic name to advantage. Finding an immediate and appreciative audience for his remarkable talents, many following him from Miettas, Reymond was soon able to move to a venue matching his aspirations, a grand 1880s mansion in Melbourne's leafy inner suburb of Prahran. In its first year of existence, Jacques Reymond was awarded the top honour of three hats in the respected *Age Good Food Guide*. Twenty-five years later and those three hats are his again. The level of consistency is extraordinary. Recently welcomed into the prestigious membership of Relais & Châteaux, an elite association of the world's finest hotels and restaurants, Reymond's stately venue remains the flagship of his diverse and extraordinary contribution to Melbourne's culinary life. After waiting for a brief moment for our reservation to be noted, it was the restaurant's maitre d' who showed us to our table. Though he was never forward enough to introduce himself, Gareth Burnett's name and South African heritage were things I already knew. Front-of-house professionals with skills to match such a fine establishment and experience necessary to lead the substantial service staff it requires are rare. Burnett's appointment to the role was noted in the press. The son of hoteliers in his home country, he moved to the United Kingdom where he trained and worked in Michelin-starred restaurants before coming to Australia. Burnett is obviously a man of high personal standards, standards he expects to be shared by all members of his staff and, perhaps, his guests. A recent and frustrated question he posed on Twitter betrayed his regard for those who fail: 'In what universe is it ok to "rock up" to a three-hatted restaurant in shorts and unbuttoned shirt?' Still, his competent and assured presence, balancing warmth

The Five-star Table

and discretion almost perfectly, lent the simple act of being seated the sense of occasion you hope for.

Settled in our corner table in the largest of the restaurant's three dining rooms – my beloved seated on a caramel-coloured leather banquette set against the wall with plush burgundy cushions either side – we looked out through the four high arched windows that ran the length of the room. A carefully tended courtyard garden fronted the house with a fountain at its centre. At both ends of the room were substantial marble fireplaces, each with an ornately framed mirror finished in gold leaf hanging grandly above. Our table was covered in crisp white linen, the generous glassware gleaming from the light of the shaded chandeliers. The cutlery, a piece of which I balanced for a moment in my hand, was Christofle Hotel, beautifully handcrafted silverware manufactured in Normandy since 1830.

In moments, though generously spaced, we had menus in our hands, glasses filled with sparkling water and two *gougeres* straight from the oven on our side plates. A generous and deliciously light puff of choux pastry and Gruyere cheese, as warmly pleasant in aroma as taste, has been a staple on Reymond's menu from the beginning. In a comforting sort of way, the smell, feel and taste of the *gougere* gave this grand and opulent space a sense of home. As for our meal, the choices were relatively simple. The majority of guests come to Jacques Reymond for the degustation, a set menu in nine courses, along with matching wines for the adventurous. A closely aligned vegetarian degustation is also available. For the less willing and perhaps more sensible, the carte is a listing of ten dishes with no division between entrees and mains. Of these smaller dishes, guests are invited to choose four, five or six courses, each option at a set price. With the distinct possibility that it may be another fourteen years before our return, we chose the degustation, my beloved taking the vegetarian route. Our waiter was clearly pleased. 'We want to take you on a journey tonight,' she said, with not a hint of hubris. 'Sit back and enjoy,' she added, 'It's a beautiful way to spend an evening. And it's one you'll not forget.'

To justly describe a meal like this with nothing but words is impossible. It certainly is for me. I run the risk of sounding like an infatuated adolescent dizzy from new love. No matter how good the description might be, fine eating is one of those things on the list titled 'You had to be there!' I can only say our waiter was right, on all counts. The meal was a journey, and from the *gougere* to the final petit four, it was one of extraordinary beauty. Indeed, it is an experience I will never forget. Along with just a handful of other meals, it will remain with me for a long time to come.

Jacques Reymond has been described as one of Australia's most consistently balanced yet daring chefs. Indeed, for me it was that blend of consistency, balance and daring – a blend that can only come from a lifetime of profound concentration on one's art – that was richly present in each and every course. From the opening serve of ocean trout in the smallest cubes, slow-cooked and smoked and resting on a consommé jelly so light yet intense in flavour, to the closing Venezuelan origin chocolate tart served with Mount Buffalo hazelnuts, a passionfruit reduction and an iced cream infused with tonka bean and Tahitian vanilla, this was a journey through new ingredients and combinations, an extraordinary level of technique, and the pure pleasure of food so beautifully conceived and prepared. From the trout it was on to Moreton Bay bugs with soba noodles, wild succulents and caramelised black vinegar. From there, John Dory with Szechuan pepper and smoked palm sugar, then Flinders Island wallaby with the most gorgeous lamb dumpling, served in its natural cooking juices. Next, venison *tataki* matched with spanner crab tossed with fresh Tasmanian wasabi, then rare Ligurian duck, honey glazed and accompanied by the most perfect pickled cherry and a little French *barbajuan*. The final savoury dish was veal fillet with a fine crust of breadcrumbs and sea urchin butter resting on a slim medallion of lard potato, and then the 'pre-dessert', a delicate parfait of white chocolate mojito interspersed with apricot, mango and strawberry and a hint of salted caramel. Followed by the chocolate tart, coffee and the most elegant line of petit fours, the feast ended with as much style and attention to detail as it began. It was perfect.

Reymond, speaking recently to the seasoned restaurant critic Rita Erlich, reflected on his age and the prospect of retirement. 'I still feel very strong,' he said, 'mentally and physically. I don't feel any sign of being tired – even during service, I love it.' 'It's not an obligation for me,' he concluded, 'It's a pleasure!' As my beloved and I walked back down the driveway of that grand mansion, blissfully unaware of just how long the night had been, it was Reymond's pleasure that we felt most deeply, a pleasure that pervaded every aspect of our evening. Even now as I reflect back on that night, it was this same pleasure, as genuine as I can imagine it to be, that each and every person we encountered took in their contribution to our meal and our 'journey'. It is this that stays with me. It was a beautiful meal and a beautiful night.

Of course, such beauty comes at a price. As I walked down the driveway in the glow of all this pleasure and perfection, feeling buoyed and cosseted by all of life's goodness, I was also four hundred and seventy-five dollars poorer. Had I enjoyed the accompanying wines with my degustation as my beloved did with hers, the cost would have well exceeded the halfway point to a grand. Whatever way you look at it, that's an exorbitant amount of money for something as simple as dinner – just one meal on one night for two people. As a world citizen and one actively engaged with services to some of the most disadvantaged people of our city, I know something of the extraordinary imbalances and exclusions of the table – local, national and global.

On the broadest scale of comparison, data from the World Health Organisation demonstrates the confronting fact that while 1.1 billion people in the world take in excessive calories, another 1.1 billion take in too few to ward off persistent and sometimes crippling hunger. As I write, I have not long returned from visiting my brother who lives and works in South-east Asia. Part of his work is with an education foundation that provides vocational training opportunities for those in the region's poorest communities, those who are unskilled and with little prospect for secure, long-term employment. Walking through villages and neighbourhoods where securing the most basic provisions of life is a daily challenge, it does not take long to sense first-hand the inequities of our global table. My nine-course degustation begins to sit uncomfortably.

Closer to home, our national table shows its own signs of division. Though Australia is a 'food secure' nation, one where food is available in abundance, somewhere between seven and ten percent of its citizens live with significant levels of food insecurity every day. This often has to do with lack of financial resources. Fresh and nutritious whole foods are sold at a premium in the suburbs. The cheaper and more accessible options are highly processed and pre-packaged foods high in fat, sugar and salt. It's why the poorer suburbs in Melbourne will have two to three times more fast-food outlets than affluent ones. Food insecurity is also greater in communities that are geographically and socially isolated. Reports from the Australian Institute of Health and Welfare show that those most likely to be obese and suffering from obesity-related diseases and the consequences of poor nutrition are those who are poor, indigenous and living well outside the nation's largest metropolitan areas. In a land of abundance and opulent tables, all is not equal.

And then there are the local inequities of the table. It is these that I find most confronting. I have only to step outside my office on Collins Street and I will see those seated inside Melbourne's numerous up-market restaurants and those seated outside on the footpaths and bench seats, those whose most expensive meal purchase might be McDonalds on a good day and the Flinders Street soup van on others. Sitting at Jacques Reymond surrounded by such rich and sumptuous expressions of life, I cannot avoid the table's exclusivity. Dining in Melbourne, from its most formal and refined to its most informal and relaxed, is one of the clearest social dividers we have.

The social divisions of the table have always been with us, but there are moments when I feel them more keenly than others. One of those was a decade ago. On a mild and grey Tuesday night in Melbourne's inner suburb of Fitzroy, I joined a small, sophisticated crowd in a bookshop nestled among the cafés of Gertrude Street. Books for Cooks has to be one of the most reassuring little places on Melbourne's literary landscape and, quite possibly, one of its best-kept secrets. With its rambling rooms morphing from one to the other, each one stocked floor to ceiling with every cookbook imaginable along with a feast of food writing and serious journals of gastronomy, this is a place of regular pilgrimage for me.

This particular night we had gathered not to peruse the bookshelves but to hear from one of the doyennes of Australian food journalism, Jill Dupliex. A Melbournian who was at the time living in London as food writer for *The Times*, Dupliex remains a prolific author and regular columnist for *Epicure*, *Gourmet Traveller* and numerous other glossy publications. As well as being articulate and thoroughly charming, she knows how to cook *and* write, a rare combination. True to form she charmed us all. I was besotted.

I was also distracted. As Jill spoke, she stood at the front of the store with the shop windows directly behind her. While listening to Jill, I could not help but see the trickle of people passing by on the footpath outside. At the time, Gertrude Street was an eclectic mix of stylish boutiques, art supplies, galleries and cafés sitting alongside graffitied factories, op shops, old pubs and abandoned storefronts with broken windows. Ten years later, Gertrude Street is on a growing list of trendy and increasingly gentrified inner-city thoroughfares that snake their way through Melbourne's inner suburbs. Its list of impossibly cool eating houses has grown while the abandoned shop fronts have all but disappeared. Still, some things haven't changed. At one end of the street lie the majestic Royal Exhibition Building and the gracious Carlton Gardens; at the other end, high-rise housing commission flats along with services for the homeless, mentally ill and unemployed. And the sidewalk benches in between are still home to those who have nowhere else to sleep.

Inside the bookshop that night we were all well dressed – uniform inner-city black for the most part, dark-rimmed glasses, suits and champagne. Distractingly, most of those who walked by outside, occasionally peering in curiously, looked markedly different: one with a bottle of Fosters in his hand, struggling to remain upright as he steadied himself against the window; another looking lost, dishevelled and clutching an old bag of newspapers. It was like two different worlds; we were 'in' and they were clearly 'out'.

For me, this experience embodied an uncomfortable truth and one that my meal at Jacques Reymond has only updated. As one who relishes the culinary sophistication of this city – its five-star or three-hat tables, food and wine festivals, and boutique food stores and markets – I cannot avoid the fact that the Melbourne table is an exclusive one. The truth is, where we eat, what we eat, and with whom is an indication of our social standing and the ever-clearer divisions in our society between those who have and those who don't. I confess that juggling those concurrent feelings of 'besotted' and 'distracted' is still a struggle. To be honest, juggling has never been my strength.

As a person of Christian faith, I am guided in life by a set of values inherent to the stories and traditions of my religion. These values impact my understanding of life and give birth to commitments that shape the way I live it. People of faith will articulate and organise such values in myriad ways. For me, the two most telling and formative commitments are those of beauty and justice.

Every Sunday as I gather with others to worship, I confess my faith in the God of creation, a God in whom I understand all beauty finds its genesis. I declare the ancient words of the psalmist extolling this majestic beauty of God and I sing the words of old hymns that tell of divine beauty in all the earth.

> For the beauty of the earth,
> for the glory of the skies,
> for the love which from our birth
> over and around us lies.
>
> For each perfect gift of Thine
> to us all so freely given,
> graces human and divine,

flowers of earth and buds of heaven.
Lord of all, to Thee we raise
this our joyful hymn of praise.
(Folliot Pierpoint, 1835–1917)

What's more, I own a faith that names this beauty as a transforming power in the world, one that I am called to behold, seek and nurture all the days of my life. For wherever I behold beauty, I behold God; wherever I seek it, I seek God; wherever I nurture it, I nurture the possibility of eternity. In essence, to be besotted by beauty is part of my spiritual calling.

At the same time my loyalty is to a God of justice, a God who, according to the sacred texts of my faith, sides with the oppressed and marginalised at every opportunity and calls me to do likewise. 'What does the Lord require of you?' the prophet asks rhetorically before answering, 'to do justice, and to love kindness, and to walk humbly with your God' (Micah 6:8). It is an unambiguous call echoed by Jesus through his actions and words: 'Just as you did it to one of the least of these ... you did it to me' (Matthew 25:40). In my theology, to turn toward human need is to turn toward God; to hear the cries of injustice and exclusion is to hear the voice of God; to embrace the poor and marginalised is to embrace the possibility of God. In fact, should I ever fail to be distracted by human need then I am likely living in a spiritually barren place. Of course, as a person of faith I hold no monopoly on values like these. Commitments to beauty and justice can be owned just as deeply by those who have no religious conviction at all. For all of us, religious or not, the challenge comes when holding beauty and justice together creates a tension difficult to manage, the moments when 'besotted' and 'distracted' pull in two directions. Granted, beauty and justice can be and often are two sides of the one extraordinary coin – those moments when you witness such beauty in an act of justice it takes your breath away, or when justice is so embodied in beauty it compels with exhilarating force – but that's not always the case. Sometimes you can feel like you're straddling two powerful currents and jumping one ship for another is the only viable option.

Food is a beautiful thing. On one hand food's beauty is commonplace, a thing we routinely brush past unaware. A bowl of summer fruit sits on the kitchen bench, a display of berries, nectarines, peaches and grapes. If I stop long enough to look, I am struck by the shape, colour and form of this still life and its organic splendour. Most often, though, like children's artworks gathered on the refrigerator door, food's beauty forms a backdrop unnoticed. On the other hand, there is the beauty of epiphany in food. There are moments when we are so struck by the sheer artistry of food well prepared that we are in the moment nourished deeply by it, even challenged to see things anew because of it. It is like entering a gallery of great art and being enveloped in a world of beauty and truth. There are gasps, tears, moments of knowing when the things of life find a new clarity or perspective. Beauty has the power to transform.

In such moments, the beauty of food might be understood as a peripheral beauty. It is the beauty of excess, the beauty found in what the architectural critic Elizabeth Farrelly calls the 'blubber' of life, all that is spare or surplus to need.

> Blubber is whale oil for the lamps on long winter nights. It's the egg's white, the fruit's flesh, the yeasty bounce of a baby's thigh ... the aedicule, gazebo or porch that adds to a building nothing but graciousness; the purposeless energy of birdsong that is neither mating call or warning but pure, simple pleasure; the spare time in the day, or in the tribal calendar, that makes space for creative play. Blubber, in this sense, is the crack where the light gets in.

Can we live without such beauty? Possibly. Do we want to? No. For we have come to know that our longing for it rests deeply within us; our yearning for the light that beauty casts cries out to be fed just as much as our tummies cry out for physical sustenance. It's why we set the table, light the candles, arrange the flowers and garnish the plates. The beauty of preparation, arrangement and ritual sustains as surely as the nutrients we spoon into our mouths.

There is a sense in which a fine restaurant, like an art gallery or concert hall, is a place where what is normally peripheral to life is made central, a context and time when beauty's volume is turned up, its taste deepened.

Many good restaurateurs aspire to such an experience for their guests and work tirelessly toward it. Sydney chef Tony Bilson is one of the few to articulate it in such explicit terms. In his autobiography *Insatiable*, Bilson describes his longing for his harbour-side dining room to be a gallery of the gastronomic arts and his role as the chef-curator of a transforming experience for those who come:

> I wanted to give my vision of contemporary cuisine to our guests and share with them the beauty that I had experienced. I wanted to create a song about the beauty of existence in their memories. A slow sensual song that would sit in their subconscious and reappear in tales told to their children and grandchildren. That's why I think the design of a restaurant is important in achieving those moments of epiphany. It allows the guest's mind to listen to the song. The final step in their experience, the music if you wish, is to compose a menu where the rhythm of food and wine seeps into the senses the same way as an Aboriginal song heard in the bush comes to symbolise the subconscious experience. The environment becomes part of the memory, the scents and the tastes integrated into subtle seduction.

These are aspirational words, heady with longing. It is this longing for beauty that permeates Bilson's story from his earliest days in the kitchen to the present. What his story illustrates, however, is the very messy and compromised business it is to curate an experience of such beauty when the companions of sensuality, the thirst for profit, the driving power of pride, and our natural bent to excess and exclusivity lurk in its shadows. While the blubber of life may provide the crack where the light gets in, it can also become an embalming shroud, a sludge in which the soul slowly drowns. The world of fine dining is as full of sludge-filled potholes as it is with vistas of beauty. Nowhere is the human bent to conspicuous excess more evident than at the tables of our finest restaurants. How easily the diner can become, to use Farrelly's words, 'blubber-rich but meaning poor', so infatuated with the possession or pursuit of the table's beauty that they no longer see it or what it points them toward.

Some will argue that the sludge of the five-star table is simply too thick, the tensions between beauty and justice too compromising. If one is in genuine pursuit of the table's spirituality, they conclude, one has no choice but to walk away from the white linen and imported tableware in pursuit of a simpler, more inclusive experience. The sociologist Joanne Finkelstein is one of those.

In her book *Dining Out*, Finkelstein writes of the 'fundamental incivility' of the restaurant meal for which there is scant hope of redemption. For the meal to be civilised, or saved, Finkelstein argues for a complete ridding of all 'hyperbole and artifice', eradicating once and for all the 'chicanery' involved in the restaurant meal's preparation and presentation. It is clear from her conclusions, however, that her hope for such purging is meagre.

Observing the transactions of restaurants, Finkelstein paints a dark and brooding picture. She points to (i) a gross imbalance of power and control, (ii) a mass of 'subaltern' desires and influences within the diner, (iii) a 'theatrical camouflaging' of what is the most basic provision of service, (iv) a 'relentless and dark pursuit' of maximum profit, (v) intentionally concealed and conflicting interests between restaurateur and diner, and (vi) the primacy of 'private expectations and desires'. As for the impact upon the diner's spirit, the fine dining experience takes its toll. According to Finkelstein, this act of routine indulgence facilitates the flourishing of things completely counter to the soul of a good society: (i) a heightened degree of social reserve and aloofness, allowing the diner to mix with others without the personal cost of direct engagement; (ii) blunted sensibilities, enabling the diner to see others as objects of desire, imitation, envy or derision; and (iii) an almost mindless conformity to social expectations, fashions and customs for the sake of blending in.

In many respects, Finkelstein is right. Indeed, this act of fine dining is a compromised business and everything she observes is there in good measure. But to so dismiss a whole sector of industry, craft, vocation and pleasure in terms like these is an extraordinary leap of logic. The description of 'subaltern influences', 'theatrical camouflaging', 'relentless

The Five-star Table

pursuit of profit', 'concealed and conflicting interests', and the 'primacy of private desires' could be made of any aspect of human industry and interaction. Even within the church, an institution with an explicitly spiritual agenda and the aspiration to move beyond such things, we are guilty as charged. What's more, the hazards of social reserve, blunted sensibilities and mindless conformity are as real among those who work with the poor as those who network on the thirty-fifth floor. The dangers and pitfalls are different but the basic human struggle is the same. In my view, it is simplistic to paint the fine-dining experience in such caricatured terms and in so doing suggest a simple choice: partake and be damned to compromise or withdraw to table nirvana. While our participation at the five-star table deserves critique, it surely deserves a more intelligent and nuanced one than that.

Hong Kong is one of my favourite cities. There are few other places where I leave feeling exhilarated and exhausted to the same degree. On my last trip I was invited to work with two different communities exploring the connections between spirituality and the workplace: at one end, company executives from large manufacturing industries, and at the other, an organisation working with street cleaners, stallholders and sex workers in one of the most densely populated and poverty-ridden regions of the city.

Along the way I was asked to give a public lecture on spirituality in the hospitality industry. People came from vocations and businesses across the sector, from hoteliers to small business owners, chefs to purveyors of fine teas. It was one of the most engaged audiences I've experienced. After the presentation I sat with Joey, a Hong Kong native of Japanese decent and the head chef at one of the city's finer restaurants, a lavish establishment hidden among the upper floors of an exclusive indoor shopping complex. With Gucci, Prada and Chanel stores alongside, its opulent interior design has been featured in the glossy pages of *Gourmet Traveller* and feted by an international clientele.

It was clear Joey loved his work. His eyes danced as he told me of his achievements, awards and aspirations. He was both passionate and proud, and rightly so. He also spoke easily of his religious faith and the seriousness with which he took his call to a life of service. 'Do you feel supported in that?' I asked him.

He looked at me blankly. 'By my church?' he answered with raised eyebrows.

'Yes,' I prodded, 'do you sense their support of your work in the kitchen?'

He laughed. 'No, they don't understand. We live in two different worlds.'

Joey told me of his church, a small community that meets in a crowded Mong Kok neighbourhood and offers support services to some of the district's poorest residents. 'I don't blame them,' Joey continued. 'I find it hard enough myself. Moving between this neighbourhood and my work is like jumping across a river every day.'

I asked him why he keeps jumping.

'I can't do it any other way,' he said with a smile. 'I've tried. I left the kitchen to work fulltime here. I only lasted six months. I felt like my right harm had been cut off. I cannot *not* cook beautiful food. I feel alive when I cook. I'm happy in a way I can't describe. It's like God is smiling.'

'But you haven't left your church behind?' I asked.

'No, I can't do that either. I still cook here every Sunday night and eat with the people in the street. It's good. To be honest, I don't like myself when I don't. These people will never come to my restaurant and they don't know about my awards. It's simpler. It's honest. There something about it I need … and they need me. It's a good deal!'

Joey's image of 'jumping the river' between the worlds of five-star dining and neighbourhood justice is a good one. It neither minimises the tension nor proffers the simplistic choices of either/or. Perhaps a bit of river jumping is essential to our life at the table, a willingness to live creatively with the tensions rather than resolving them. That said, our pursuit of a spirituality of the table that values both beauty and justice calls more for action than resignation.

In my own river jumping, I have found encouragement in the perspectives of the North American theologian J. Shannon Jung. In his book *Food for Life*, Jung argues that the real joy of food – the delight of the table whatever form it takes – is only found and maintained when we are aware of food's *source* and *purpose*. In Jung's language, *food's source is God*. It is a gift, given to us from a source beyond our own making, and through eating we express our dependence upon that source. It's a good reminder that food in its most organic form does not originate in the supermarket, nor does it magically appear as a consequence of our purchasing power. It is certainly not the creation of a chef, no matter how talented. It's not even the product of a farmer's hard work. Before it is anything else food is grace, a gift of the earth that sustains and strengthens our lives.

Secondly, according to Jung, *food's purpose is in sharing*. Food is given for relationship. It's why the table is so important to food. The table is an expression of our community, a place to acknowledge our mutual humanity and need. It's not just a family or local table; it's a global one. Their global character is what makes the experiences of poverty and hunger so dehumanising. When those at this end of the table have food in abundance while those at that end have barely enough to survive, we are all diminished. The truth is, food is the great leveller. It is our common need, and it's made to share.

It is with these two principles in mind that I have come to live with the 'besotted' and 'distracted' tensions of my table life, not in a way that resolves them but with a greater sense of resolve. Firstly, *I am resolved to embrace whatever beauty my life at the table provides with a conscious sense of gratitude*. It is a choice to receive my daily food, be it in a fine restaurant or on a park bench, with thankfulness and respect. Delight comes in acknowledgement: this is not deserved; it is a gift. The old religious practice of 'grace' before meals is one of acknowledgement and delight, a routine pause every time food is placed before me to name my dependence and my gratitude. It's also a practice of humility, a reminder that the abundance before me is not a marker of my personal success or my cultural superiority to those who have less. It is certainly not the thing that separates me into a protected corral of affluence. Rather, genuine delight is found in the sense of grace and blessing that is mine through food and in the complex web of interdependence it represents. While I may not dine at Jacques Reymond very often, when I do I will do so with an unbridled sense of delight. When that is not the case, I'll know it's time to stay home.

Secondly, *I am resolved to live a life at the table that is as committed to justice and inclusion as it is to beauty and abundance.* The philosopher Roger King has said that our eating practices can either 'obscure the world or help to make it visible'. Wherever I eat, I want to do so with eyes open not closed, in ways that connect not hide. For me, that means ensuring that I am sitting as often with those excluded and marginalised by our table life as I am with those who are as comfortable and affluent as I am. From a logistical perspective, that is not difficult for me. I work in a building where opportunities to eat with the poor are mine on tap. What's more, the city streets I walk each day are home to the familiar faces and stories of those who live there, hand to mouth, and with whom I can talk, pass time and share food as often as I choose: people like Louis with his preference for the most minimal personal space and his penchant for McDonalds cheeseburgers, or Ryan whose vigorous handshakes always lead to a 'Lord of the Fries' feast for two.

From a more personal perspective, the choice for justice and inclusion in my table life is one I have to make and remake daily. To be honest, it is easier to live with the world obscured; the sharing of resources never comes as easily as the spending of them. Delighting in the beauty of five stars will always come more naturally than investing in the justice of none. But I am resolved.

◆ RECIPE

Raspberry and White Chocolate Pavlova

When it comes to the beauty pageant of food, raspberries take to the marble-topped runway with a style and simplicity hard to match. Trouble is, these delicate gems are as small as they are magnificent and can roll by without being noticed (or get squashed in the rush). Rest one in your hand, though; behold its intricacy, shape and colour, and there's no doubt that a single raspberry is an object of the most natural, even complex beauty. Piled atop the white peaks of a thick, rich cream, an unadorned mound of these fragile little things is breathtaking.

I'm not much for cooking with raspberries. It always seems a waste. Raspberry jam, raspberry crumble, raspberry coulis: all legitimate in their own way, and often delicious, but the berry's visual delight is sacrificed. It's why I like the use of raspberries that lets them be and allows them to shine as they are. This recipe for raspberry-topped pavlova with a sprinkling of white chocolate does just that, providing a base that sweetens and highlights the visual carnival these berries provide. It's also a mixture of textures and tastes that works: the sweet plumpness of the fruit, the smoothness of the cream and the crunch of the pavlova with the marshmallow hidden below. The fact that the 'pav' sits securely within the Australian food canon certainly adds to its virtue. Given the brevity of the raspberry season, the opportunities for this glorious display are limited, but worth the wait.

Ingredients
- 4 egg whites, best at room temperature
- 250 grams of castor sugar
- 2 teaspoons of cornflour
- 1 teaspoon of vinegar
- 1 teaspoon of vanilla essence
- 300 ml of cream
- 2 punnets (or 3) of raspberries, in season. Don't bother with the frozen or canned varieties. Really, eat a Cherry Ripe instead!
- Good-quality white chocolate for shaving

Method
- Pre-set the oven to 180°C and line a baking tray with a circle of baking paper.
- Whisk the egg whites (preferably in an electric mixer) until natural peaks form.
- Add the castor sugar, a little at a time, and keep whisking until the mixture is firm and shiny in texture.
- Add the cornflour, vinegar and vanilla, and fold them in gently by hand.
- Spoon the mixture onto the baking paper and, with a spatula, shape it into a circle approximately 20cm across, flattening the top and smoothing the sides as best you can. Remember that it needs to look a bit 'blobby' so don't go for perfection.
- Place it in the oven, reducing the heat to 140°C immediately, and cook for an hour and a quarter.
- Turn the oven off and leave the pavlova to cool in the oven with the door closed. Overnight is good.
- Once the pavlova is completely cooled, shift it carefully from the baking paper to a platter or, even better, a lovely white cake pedestal (I like them!).
- Using a grater, shave off several spoonfuls of white chocolate.
- Whisk the cream until it's thick and spoon it on top of the pavlova, spreading it out as evenly as you can manage.
- Now pile the raspberries on top and sprinkle over the white chocolate shavings. Stand back and gasp at your genius, and then hoe in!

CHAPTER 6

The Work Table
Eating, Cooking and Vocation

It's midnight. Changed out of his whites into jeans and a pullover, James stands at the doorway of the kitchen leading out into the deserted restaurant courtyard. Behind him, the familiar sound of empty bottles being tipped into a recycling bin, and in front, the residue of another busy night all but cleaned away. It's been good for a Tuesday. About one hundred and twenty covers in all; not bad for a place that seats just sixty. Given the business is only seven months old, things are going well. The kitchen has found its pace and is humming along nicely. Even the service staff are settling down after some early tensions. Two good reviews in the city's newspapers have made a huge difference.

James pulls on his coat and heads out the front door. He stops on the footpath to chat briefly with Georgie, one of the service staff sitting alone in the cold with her cigarette. Normally the conversation would linger flirtatiously, but not tonight. After a few moments James says goodbye and heads off into the darkness of another bleak winter night. Usually he walks home, about twenty-five minutes from door to door. Tonight he's tired and hails a passing taxi.

Just ten minutes later James is at the door of a small worker's cottage in the inner-city suburb of Collingwood, a place he shares with his brother. He fumbles with his keys then closes the door behind him. After a shower and an almost liturgical flick through the television channels, James falls asleep on the couch, his mind and body weary from a fifteen-hour day.

It's not easy work, but it's all he's known since leaving school twelve years ago. On deck six nights a week and lunches for four of those days, James' working hours are long. Time for relationships outside of the restaurant is almost non-existent. Still, he loves what he does and has never imagined it any other way.

James and I meet the next day during a late afternoon break. The opportunity to talk was arranged by a mutual friend and we sit together at Brunetti, an outdoor café in Melbourne's city square. Though it doesn't take long in a conversation to feel James' ambition and energy, it's not the first thing I notice. He has an easy-going charm, disarmingly so, matched by a broad, open smile. James is a country boy, having grown up in Shepparton in central Victoria. Intrigued by my interest in his work, he's happy to chat and does so easily.

At twenty-nine, James has been working in Melbourne's restaurant industry since leaving school and heading to the city at seventeen. Though he fell into his first job as 'a general dog's body' in a suburban bistro – because there was nothing else on offer – cooking soon caught his imagination. It's now a career he takes seriously. Securing an apprenticeship at eighteen, James has worked in some of Melbourne's better-known restaurants and cafés. He even did a brief stint in one of the city's five-star hotels but prefers the more personal feel of an 'independent'. 'Things are less by-the-card,' he says, 'It's more creative and working up a loyal customer base makes it a challenge.'

Despite his laid-back air, James has no difficulty describing his plans for the future. Most immediately, they include having a restaurant of his own by the time he's thirty-two. His 'partner in crime' is Raffi, an erratic but gifted pastry chef, originally from El Salvador, who has moved with him the last three years. Ever the enthusiast, Raffi says he's committed to the same vision, though James quietly suspects his focus will wain before then: 'Let's just say he's inspired more by his groin than his head!' Like many in the industry, Raffi maintains the pace with a potent blend of

The Work Table

alcohol and whatever stimulants are available. 'His desserts are sublime,' James says, 'and when he's good he's really good, but when he's bad he's fucked-up.'

His last words create a moment of awkwardness. Realising the language he's used, James blushes. "Oh I'm sorry,' he says, leaning forward with an embarrassed grin, 'I guess I shouldn't say that to a priest, hey?' I assure him I'm not offended, and that while I'm not technically a priest, it's close enough. James tells me he was raised a Catholic and still maintains a relationship, though occasional, with his local parish. Most of his friends from the Catholic school – the place where James struggled his way through to the end of year eleven – have walked away from the church, but James says he can't. His dad's influence has been considerable. Though James' father often despaired of his son's prospects as he stumbled his way through school, James says his dad never stopped believing that he could make something of his life, something that would make a difference not just in his own world but in the world of others. 'I'm not sure how I do that in the kitchen, not in this place,' James says to me, 'unless I leave it behind and go run a soup kitchen or something. I dunno.'

As we while away an hour together in the fleeting afternoon sun, I get the clear impression that this question of purpose is a nagging one for James. His older cousin Peter, he tells me, left Melbourne last year to take up a voluntary post with Médecins Sans Frontières in East Africa.

'I really respect that,' James says. 'It's like he's found something that really matters. The brothers at school used to talk about having a vocation in your life, like a calling or something. I didn't get it then, but I look at Peter and get that now. That's what he's got.' James pauses to take a sip from his coffee, looks at me, and then says in a quieter tone, 'It's really good what he's doing.'

James' last words hang in the air for a moment. I am fascinated by this concept of the 'good' and what constitutes good work, especially for those in the restaurant and café sector. It's a burgeoning market in Australia, but a notoriously challenging one to work in with a high attrition rate; indeed, the fourth highest exit rate of all Australian industries. What's more, it's a sector whose top end – the one dedicated professionals like James gravitate to – is easily caricatured and dismissed as pandering to the socially elite.

I prod, 'So what's *good* about your work, James?' I fully expect him to look at me blankly, as most people do with such a vague question.

But James hardly pauses, 'I reckon there's a lot that's good.' He sits up in his seat, as though reengaged after a passing moment of doubt. 'I mean, when it's all said and done, I feed people. And you gotta eat to live, right? Yeah, I make it look bloody good, but I feed people. That's a good thing, isn't it?' I nod in agreement

However we dress it up – and we certainly dress it well these days – a professional cook's role is to serve one of the most primary human needs. James is right: whatever else is going on when a cook does his or her work, there is a basic goodness to this simple act of feeding people. In his book *The Soul of a Chef*, Michael Ruhlman observes closely the work of several notable chefs in North America. One of those is Thomas Keller, best known for his internationally acclaimed restaurant The French Laundry in California's Napper Valley. In his closing remarks on Keller's astounding career, Ruhlman writes:

> Keller, in his twenty-five years as a chef, I guessed, had fed one million people. Probably more. This was a good thing. He was a good, thoughtful cook. The work had provided him a livelihood. It had made him famous in food circles in his country and beyond. But more important than that, and this was everything, it was the good use of one life, and he knew it.

According to Socrates, 'the good life' is discovered in the congruence between my actions and moral commitments. The good use of a life is a life lived as much for the sake of others as for myself. Basic to cooking, professional or domestic, is an act of self-giving. It's an act of service.

'When I was growing up, my mum cooked for me every night of my life,' James says. 'I didn't appreciate it then, but I do now. When she fed me she loved me. She was not always big on saying it, but she showed me when she cooked. And that's what I do, too, when I cook.' James pauses, as though to consider his own statement. 'I know it's different, but it's also the same. I don't even know the people I cook for. God knows who they are! But when I cook for them there's this connection between us. To feed people, it's intimate ... it's personal.'

In her beautiful book *Plenty*, the acclaimed Australian chef Gay Bilson – now one the country's most intelligent food writers – reflects on this odd connection between cook and diner, a distant but mutually personal relationship. Bilson recalls her early years in the groundbreaking Sydney restaurant Bon Goût that she and then husband Tony Bilson ran in the 1970s. They were heady and exciting days, and exhausting for a young mother.

> I'd finish plating desserts and baking soufflés in the Kookaburra, with Jordan in a papoose on my back, then clean up and sit on the laundry bags. In retrospect I see this connecting space as the one I never left, mentally or emotionally, in twenty-five years of running restaurants and cooking. It is the space still connected to the work and the working staff but edging towards the audience, towards a need for recognition. I didn't always sit there in contentment in those days, but there was that marvellously satisfying sense of fatigue and completion that all professional cooks, brilliant, middling or bad, understand and which seems sometimes to be what one works for.

Later she adds:

> What I learned on my naive feet was that the reward given to people who cook well and who do so with spirit and generosity and, in the best way, intelligence, is an enormous affection and gratitude. The cook in turn feels the same towards her diners, for she cannot cook without someone to cook for.

'What else is good?' I ask James as he watches the invading sparrows devour the left over muffin on the table next to us.

'I reckon a good restaurant is a place where everyone is equal,' James says, as though kicking back into gear. 'Everyone is welcome. As long as you've got a plastic card in your pocket you can come in and eat, whether you're the pope or just the bloke from the local servo.' James smiles broadly as if delighted with his own thought. 'My dad always drilled that into me when I was a kid,' he continues, 'that no matter who a bloke is or where he comes from, he deserves respect. I reckon when you cook for people that's what you do; you respect them. I mean, when we're in the middle of a really full-on service and the orders are coming in fast, we're not worried about who's getting what. We just want every plate that goes out of the kitchen to be as good as the last. Everyone gets the best!'

Interestingly, the food journalist Stephen Downes made a similar point about Australia's fine-dining scene more than a decade ago. In his book *Advanced Australian Fare*, Downes explored the evolution of the Australian restaurant scene from a culinary backwater to one of extraordinary creativity and international standing. Downes describes as 'a singular achievement' what he calls Australia's 'democratisation of fine eating out' which elsewhere remains 'an elite hobby'. While more recent critiques of Australia's eating habits would call into question Downes' generous view, I have personally found James' attitude to his work a common one among hospitality professionals. Perhaps the unique traditions of Australian culture have impacted upon our commercial kitchens and those who work in them, if not always upon the ongoing accessibility of their tables.

As James talks, his pace and energy increase. 'And I reckon a good restaurant – I mean a good one, 'cause there's lot of shit ones around – a good restaurant is a happy place.' 'I don't mean like Disneyland or something,' James almost blushes at the potential silliness of what he has just said: 'I mean it's a good place to be. It's a place where people can forget the crap in their lives, at work or whatever, and just have a good time. It's a place where they'll be treated with respect, they'll be surrounded by friends, they'll be served really good food and have plenty to drink.

'You should see our place when it's full,' James says as he leans in, 'It's like, when the rush is over, the last plates have gone out and I stand at the bar and look out at everyone having a good time, people talking and laughing, you just wouldn't want to be anywhere else.' James leans back

The Work Table

in his seat and says with that broad smile, 'It's like you get to give people a party every night. It's that good!'

James' words are mirrored in the sentiments of many professional cooks. One is fellow Melburnian Cath Claringbold, best known for her creative adaptation of Middle Eastern cuisine that first flourished in the Southbank and Docklands restaurants Mecca and Mecca Bah. In 2006, food journalist Liz Porter told the story of Claringbold's career and her love for what she does. Porter writes:

> Claringbold pours herself another glass of water and looks out the Mecca Bah window onto the water as smooth and slate grey as the winter sky. 'My favourite view is the other way,' she says, turning back and looking at the tables of customers spooning out tagine from colourful dishes imported from Tunisia. 'I love the thrill of the pressure. It comes from having gone through a really big service, where you are doing anything from 180 to 200 covers a night, and knowing that most of the meals have gone out and you've been proud of them. You write a menu, and you hope people will come. Then you work really hard, and have a great night and everyone's happy – it's like having a great dinner party.'

Isak Dinesen's acclaimed short story *Babette's Feast*, adapted so beautifully for the 1987 Academy Award-winning film by the same name, is the tale of two elderly and pious sisters, Martine and Philippa, living in a remote and isolated corner of Denmark's Jutland in the late nineteenth century. The sisters, who struggle to maintain a declining religious sect founded by their late father, unwittingly provide sanctuary for Babette Hersant, a political refugee fleeing counter-revolutionary bloodshed in France. Though they know nothing about her, they accept her offer to serve as their cook and housekeeper in exchange for nothing but a room and bed. For the next fourteen years Babette toils quietly in the background, retaining her anonymity and providing for the sisters' very basic needs.

On the occasion of the centenary of their late father's birth, the sisters plan a modest supper for the remaining elderly and fractious members of the sect. Babette seeks the sisters' permission to provide a 'real French dinner' for the occasion. The sisters give their hesitant approval. Little do they know that Babette will spend the entire proceeds from a lottery win, ten thousand francs, on ingredients especially imported from France and prepare a dinner of the most sublime beauty.

At the end of this meal – a wondrously transformative event for those who gather – the sisters discover that their Babette is in reality one of Paris's most acclaimed and gifted chefs of the esteemed restaurant Café Anglais. When the dinner is over and the guests have departed blissfully into the night, the sisters find Babette sitting exhausted in her kitchen surrounded by the debris of the feast. She explains to them that in Paris she had cooked for the very people from whom she fled fourteen years earlier, and for them she still grieves:

> You see, Mesdames ... those people belonged to me, they were mine. They had been brought up and trained, with greater expense than you, my little ladies, could ever imagine or believe, to understand what a great artist I am. I could make them happy. When I did my very best I could make them perfectly happy.

In his masterful book *The Pudding That Took a Thousand Cooks*, food historian Michael Symons provides a wonderful affirmation of the role cooks play, past and present, in drawing people together in relationship. At their best – as James, Cath and Babette understand – cooks are hosts, facilitators of something even more significant than the food they prepare. Of restaurants like James', Symons writes:

> Some diners come to escape. Some diners come to flaunt their wealth, their fashionability, their good taste. Many also come to forge and affirm commercial alliances, to celebrate anniversaries, to discharge obligations, to court. They come to talk, to exchange, to win. But, at a deeper level even than sharing lives, all diners come to share food. In getting us together, cooks sustain social liaisons. Cooks hold us in bonds and networks – with the world and one another.

James is just one of the estimated one hundred thousand professional cooks that serve in Australia's restaurants, cafés and hotels every day of the week. Certainly not everyone in the industry is as articulate or ambitious as he is. There are countless cooks, waiters and bar tenders for whom work is nothing more than a way to make ends meet or an unwelcome pit stop on the way to something else. But within the industry are men and women for whom their work and dreams collide somewhere between the service of lunch and dinner. 'Dreams drive hospitality,' chef and writer Jim Hearne says of Australia's restaurants and cafés. Indeed, given the challenge of turning a sustainable profit in today's eating houses – the cold fact is ninety percent of restaurants are closed before the end of their second year – the dream plays a much more significant motivating role than a good business plan will ever do.

James recalls the brothers from his Catholic school talking easily of 'vocations' and 'callings' and their importance to our lives. Indeed, according to their origins these are distinctly religious terms. The word 'vocation' comes from the Latin *vocare*, meaning 'to call', and was used first in Middle English to interpret the ancient biblical language of divine calling – a call from God to be someone, to do something, or to go somewhere. Still today people like me, those in a religious profession, use the language of 'calling' with ease. Elsewhere it's close to non-existent. Even among those who claim a religious faith, telling people you are 'called' can sound, at best, a bit too mystical or grandiose for the average pew sitter, and at worst, akin to a night-time visit from aliens. The word 'vocation' is less problematic. Talk of 'vocational guidance' or 'vocational counselling' is commonplace. Free from its explicitly religious confines, vocation still carries with it something more than just employment: the simple exchange of human labour for monetary reward. To speak of a vocation is to describe a deeper matching of work with our passions, commitments, gifts and dreams.

In my own conversations with people like James, I am routinely surprised by the deeper motivations that inspire the work of professional cooks, those who invest their lives in restaurant kitchens. While dreams may drive the opening of new businesses, it is deeper, more lasting dreams that routinely inspire the work that sustains them. Those dreams can be birthed early on, before one ever dons a white hat and apron, or materialise along the way and without planning as they did for James.

Regardless, these dreams of identity, passion, longing – obsessions with excellence, cravings for recognition, the driven pursuit of success or beauty or connection – are tangible at kitchen workbenches the world over.

In his autobiography *The Apprentice*, the Frenchman Jacques Pépin, apprenticed at thirteen to La Grande Hôtel de l'Europe in Paris, tells the story of his rise from the family restaurant in rural France to culinary celebrity in the United States. Pépin describes his boyhood passion for cooking and his early sense of destiny in the kitchen, a sense that his older brother Roland did not share.

> One night, after we had collapsed into bed after scrubbing the last pot, Roland confided, 'I don't want to live this life when I grow up, Tati. I don't want to work anywhere near a kitchen.' Lying beside him in the dark, I thought about what he had said. It had never dawned on me that there was another life – certainly not for a Pépin. I loved the very things Roland dreamed of escaping, the hurly-burly noise of the kitchen. The heat. The sweat. The bumping of bodies. The raised voices. The constant rush of adrenaline. I loved going to the market in the morning, hurrying back, and, if it wasn't a school day, frantically preparing the food we had purchased, finishing just as the first customers came in for lunch. I loved sitting around the big table in the restaurant after the service, eating with my mother, my father, my brothers, the two waitresses, and the dishwasher. I belonged.

Pépin later describes his experience, early in his apprenticeship, of being 'called to the stove'. For Pépin, once he had learned the basics, this call was a significant rite of passage – akin to the religious rite of confirmation in his Catholic faith. While few professional cooks could tell a similar story of destiny and calling combined, and in such religious terms, there is more commonly a sense of epiphany, a moment of discovery related to the kitchen. This was certainly the case for James.

'I remember walking into the cold store in that bistro when I was seventeen and thinking "Whoa!",' James says. 'It was amazing … the colours, the smells, and the volume … it was beautiful. Endless possibility. Like this whole new world inside a fridge! I had never seen

The Work Table

anything like it!' It was a similar experience for Cath Claringbold, 'just a red-headed girl from Bacchus Marsh', who fell into cooking via a casual roadhouse job on the Western Highway making burgers. From there she scored a cooking apprenticeship at the Victorian Arts Centre and then, craving a job in a 'real restaurant', badgered her way into one of Melbourne's finest of its day, Slattery's. When Claringbold first entered the tiny kitchen, it was love at first sight: 'I had never seen anything like it before,' Claringbold says. 'The incredible sourdough starters that made the most gorgeous breads. French cheeses, homemade icecreams. Parmigiano-reggiano, gorgeous smoked bacon – produce that I had never tasted before.' The notorious Englishman Gordon Ramsey tells the same tale to journalist Simon Wright. Upon the commencement of his 'apprenticeship' with the renowned Marco Pierre White, Ramsey speaks of a spiritual homecoming: 'I walked into that kitchen, I thought my God. We've gone from twenty-five to thirty cooks in a kitchen to like four ... This guy was boning out pigeons, he was chopping shallots, picking the spinach, he was making tagliatelle and it was like, Jesus this is me, I've found my base. I've found me. I wanted it.'

Epiphanies and obsessions in the kitchen often go hand-in-hand. That is certainly true in the world of fine food. And where there is obsession, there is invariably a deeper spirituality at play. One of the most celebrated culinary obsessives was the Frenchman Bernard Loiseau, the larger-than-life, irrepressible and entirely likeable star of late twentieth-century French gastronomy. He was one of the culinary elite, awarded the prestigious three stars by the Michelin Guide for his restaurant La Côte d'Or in rural France. Indeed, to be so rewarded was Loiseau's life ambition. However, according to Rudolph Chelminski's remarkable biography, Loiseau was dogged by an unrecognised and untreated bipolar disorder. His professional highs were matched only by his emotional lows. Under the captivating veneer of bravado and self-promotion, Loiseau lived in perpetual fear of failure. Tragically, in the early months of 2003 and at the height of his career – panicked by the unfounded rumour of his demotion to just two stars – Loiseau took his own life. His devoted wife Dominique found him in their bedroom with the gun by his side.

From Chelminski's account, Loiseau was a perfectionist of the highest order, an obsessive-compulsive totally consumed by his culinary vision. In his infatuation with what proved to be ultimately elusive, Loiseau allowed everything else in his life to take a back seat. Obsessions like this are easy to caricature and even easier to critique. Yet, truth be told, without them our world would be a poorer place. One cannot help but be captivated by this man's passion and absolute persistence. Food was his world, and the perfecting of his art – one of creation and service in equal parts – was a pursuit of religious dimensions.

In a country not given to quite the level of infatuation that the French have for their culinary stars, Stephanie Alexander is as close to a household name in Australia as a cook can be. For close to two decades she sat at the pinnacle of the nation's gastronomical sphere, leading the restaurant that bore her name to international acclaim. Today her tome-like guide to home cooking, *The Cook's Companion*, is nothing short of a publishing phenomenon, and her work to establish kitchen gardens and education programs in schools across the nation has won extraordinary levels of community and government support. In her autobiography, one of the most honest and insightful of its genre, Alexander speaks frankly of what her success required of her and the cost she bore:

> This story should not be about Stephanie's Restaurant but about my life. But for the next seventeen years Stephanie's Restaurant was my life. The pressure and the challenge of trying to create something so special meant that everything else became subordinate. It was not that I did not value my family and friends – I absolutely needed them. But I could not find a way of managing and operating the restaurant without it sucking every gram of energy from me ... I had set myself an all-consuming task ... Every waking moment was filled with activity. There was never time to stop and reflect on priorities, or attempt to slow down. I couldn't stop.

Though the cost to Stephanie and those she loved was indeed high, and though there are tinges of uncertainty and melancholy in her reflections, this is no testimonial of regret. For one has the clear sense that Stephanie knows what every chef of her standing knows: to succeed at this level, obsession is a non-negotiable.

No doubt, in the stories of chefs like these there are pathologies to be named. But we dare not critique without understanding that real success in the culinary world, like multiple other worlds, requires nothing short of everything. As a seasoned teacher of spirituality, I know that the dominant images of spiritual centredness are those of balance, harmony, stillness and peace. But kitchens aren't like that, and those who work in them, successfully and to our benefit, do so at considerable cost. In the closing chapter of his book *The Making of a Chef*, the much acclaimed Luke Mangan concludes with words of advice to those who aspire to success in the kitchen: 'If you fall off the treadmill, pick yourself up and start running again.'

In this age of celebrity chefs and instant fame, when fully formed artists appear magically on our screens and in our restaurants as though from nowhere, we do well to remind ourselves as consumers that what we see is only the shiny tip of the iceberg. What lies underneath are lifetimes of obsession, hard work and dedication. It is a commitment as much to craft as it is to profit, as much to beauty and perfection as it is to fame and fortune. In Chelminski's words:

> Certainly, restaurants are businesses engaged in seeking profit, but it is remarkable how often they can be something very much like a calling, how often that artisans engaged in that calling are stricken by the artist's imperative to transcend the dreadful, passionless bottom-line mentality that more generally rules the modern world. It's an odd kind of business, taking money to give pleasure, but no one who has spent time observing these artisans ... can doubt for an instant the utter sincerity with which the best of them approach their craft.

I have referred already to the work of food journalist Stephen Downes. The bulk of his book *Advanced Australian Fare* is given to surveying the contributions of men and women who shaped Australia's earliest efforts at fine food: names like Hermann Schneider, Beppi Polesi, Cheong Liew, Tony Bilson, Jacques Reymond, and many more. More recently, Rita Erlich has provided something similar in her fascinating *Melbourne by Menu*, a focus on the 1980s as a pivotal decade in the development of Melbourne's food culture. What stands out as you read these stories is the depth of intelligence in so many of those who have played a key role in the Australian kitchen. It's an alternative intelligence, very different to the one we applaud and honour most loudly today. Almost to a person, these chefs were high school or university dropouts. They either did not thrive in traditional educational establishments or could not see the relevance of this learning to what they knew to be important. Yet what they went on to achieve was extraordinary. Not only so, but in talking with Downes and Erlich, they are able to articulate in the most captivating ways what it is they aspired to, were committed to and believed in. These were men and women for whom life at the culinary workbench was a vocation.

As I conclude my conversation with James and our cups sit empty on the table, he stands to shake my hand. It's the firm grip of a boy from the farm matched by that smile reaching from ear to ear. I thank him for his time: 'It's been really helpful, James. For a bloke who's just twenty-nine, you're a wise man!'

He blushes and looks down. 'Just a boy from Shep!' he says, his smile intact.

'I wish you well, James.'

'Yeah, thanks mate. You too.' With that he turns and walks away, ready to begin another shift.

◆ R E C I P E

Anna's *Baumkuchen*

My own professional days in the kitchen were short-lived compared to many in the industry, but they were formative. As an apprentice, I was trained in patisserie by Anna, an extraordinary German pastry cook who suffered fools with barely veiled disdain. As a young apprentice, I fit the 'fool' category well. Anna was a formidable woman, and she despaired openly and routinely of my ineptitude. In the earliest days I was afraid of her, but it was clear she knew how to cook and I was determined enough to keep showing up. As the years passed we moved from enemies to friends. I grew in competence and she softened. Of the many secrets Anna passed on, she taught me how to make a *baumkuchen*, or in English, a tree cake.

A tree cake is a time-consuming business. The mixture is wet, full of butter and ground nuts, and cooked in layers, each layer painted with a pastry brush into the base of a cake tin and browned under a grill. The first layer cools and then another layer is carefully painted onto the first, then grilled again. Slowly, layer by layer, the cake grows. The finished product is then wrapped in foil and set aside for at least a week to moisten. Finally, it is covered in a thin blanket of glossy chocolate icing. Cutting into it when its finished is the best part, the thin layers distinct yet working together to make the whole.

I made a *baumkuchen* recently for a significant birthday of mine and was reminded again what a beautiful thing it is. I suspect others wonder at my respect for such a cake, but I cannot separate the cake from what I know of it. I have learned first-hand what goes into it each time it's made: the care, the history and expertise, the cultural heritage, the time and patience to learn its craft.
As another year turned over in my life, it reminded me that real character is never immediate or shallow. It builds, layer upon layer. Like the layers of my tree cake, true character is accumulative, a consequence of so many daily choices to act out of love rather than selfishness, daily responses of kindness and tenderness, and routine decisions for truth.

Ingredients

Cake
- 330 grams of softened butter
- 330 grams of sugar
- Finely grated rind of one lemon
- 7 eggs
- A dash of rum or brandy
- 100 grams of crushed nuts
- 160 grams of cornflour
- 160 grams of plain flour

Icing
- 30 grams of copha
- 300 grams of icing sugar
- 30 grams of cocoa

Method
- In an electric mixer, beat together the butter, sugar and lemon rind for a good fifteen minutes.
- While still beating, add the eggs one at a time. Between the addition of each egg, be sure to combine the mixture thoroughly before adding the next one.
- Add the rum, nuts, cornflour and flour, and mix together for a further few minutes.
- Grease a 20cm round cake tin.
- With a pastry brush, add sufficient cake mix to cover the bottom of the pan as if making a pancake. Place the tin under a salamander or grill and cook until the mixture sets and browns nicely.
- Remove from the grill and add another thin layer of cake mix. Continue with the same grilling process until all the mixture is used. Don't walk away from the grill while you're cooking. Each layer will grill quite quickly and you don't want any layers burnt.

- Let the cake cool and then tip it out. Cover with foil and place in a cool, dark place for at least a few days, a week at best.
- Remove the cake from the foil and place it on a cake platter.
- Melt the copha, add the icing sugar and sifted cocoa, and mix well. The icing should be sufficiently runny to move over the entire cake without too much persuasion. A little extra water can be added if necessary.
- Cover the cake, both top and sides with the icing. It should be a very thin blanket that covers the whole cake.
- Put the cake aside for a few hours at least for the icing to set well. Don't refrigerate and don't rush.
- With a good sharp knife, cut the cake into small wedges or pieces ready to eat. Be sure to hold your first piece up; notice the layers and admire your accomplishment. As it's quite a dense and sweet cake, smaller pieces are always better. Too much of a good thing is ... too much!

CHAPTER 7

The Festive Table
Eating, Celebrating and Mourning

The food at wedding receptions has a certain taste. It's the taste of 'warm', a blandness that is neither offensive nor committed. Invariably, a typical Australian nuptial feast includes an alternating menu of 'beef or chicken', though it's rarely a choice made by the guest. I have come to accept it as predestination on a plate, though determined more by gender than divine arrangement: breast for the women, rump for the men. Large-scale cooking processes are kinder to fowl than beast, however, and being of the 'red-blooded' gender, my only hope for a swap is in my beloved's gastronomical ambivalence. Which is more rare than my beef.

At the appropriate moment in the proceedings, a pleasant young waiter with a black bow tie will reach around and place a warmed plate on the white linen in front of me. It's a place already littered with breadcrumbs from the small white roll I've devoured while listening intently to the extended life story of the groom's uncle from country Victoria, already well lubricated and seated beside me. He is either especially glad to be placed next to 'the Reverend', or mortified by the prospect, nervously filling his glass and hoping desperately I don't ask him the date of his last confession.

As a minister of religion, I've celebrated my share of wedding ceremonies (one hundred and three at last count) and alternative rituals for those to whom marriage is unavailable. And along the way I've attended more matrimonial feasts than can be good for me. Purpose-built venues are common, reception centres with romantic names like Camelot, Rose Court or The Willows. But I've also picnicked with pâté and champagne on a steep hillside as storm clouds threatened, feasted on a spit roast and foiled potatoes in a converted and pungent shearing shed, stood in an old church hall with a cup of tea and asparagus rolls, dined in a grand hotel ballroom with a thousand of the bride's closest friends, and sat around a family table with just a handful of others to toast the happy couple. Whichever way it's done, a covenant bond between two people is simply not final without a feast.

The elements of the wedding feast are important. Feasting and tradition are joined at the belly and separation is painful. That said, the traditions of the feast are odd things. With the passing of time, we may scratch our collective heads wondering where on earth they came from, while all the while embracing them with increasing flourish. Universally, ingredients essential to nuptial feasts include those that symbolise fertility, prosperity and happiness. Seeds, fruits, nuts, eggs and lashings of sugar – all essential to the traditional wedding cake encased in a sweet, white and tightly-tucked blanket of icing – are items common to marriage feasts the world over, as are things that are round and plump. Like the French croquembouche – a pyramid of little round choux balls held together with sweet and sticky caramel – the roundness of the wedding cake is a symbol of the sun and of the fertile belly of the bride. When something is round it is both open and fulsome, like the platters on which the Chinese traditionally serve the thirty-two dishes (at minimum) essential to the wedding feast, carefully balancing the yin and yang of textures and flavours: hot and cold; sweet and sour. A life of balance and prosperity is assured.

Of course, once the tables have been set and the menu prepared, it's the gathering that makes the feast, and the more the merrier. In preparation for the big day, I routinely sit with couples feeling defeated by the restrictions and permutations of their guest list. Balancing the expectations of parents, extended families, colleagues and friends creates a debilitating depth of seating-plan insomnia. And then there are others who have no such problems. My friend Seshu, who now lives and works in Melbourne, is about to head back to his home country of India. He is to be married to a young woman he has known since childhood but with whom he has rarely spoken. He is both nervous and excited. His parents, the architects of this alliance, have invited more than one thousand five hundred guests to the feast. He must depart soon and return to his Mumbai neighbourhood so that he has time to hand-deliver the invitations to each of the guests. Putting them in the post is not an option. Seshu must speak to each of the invitees in person to tell them how honoured he will be by their presence. The feast itself will be a major feat of organisation, with guests being seated in shifts and their meal – a pungent display of greens, dahls, rices, meats and condiments – served on banana leaves.

Feasting is such an important part of life's rhythms and relationships that it is difficult to imagine any major or minor alliance, rite of passage or celebration, not marked by the sharing of food and drink, and often in copious amounts. Indeed, if relationships make the world go round, it's food and drink that lubricate the cogs.

From the very beginnings of human society, we have ritualised our celebrations. Feasting and ritual are a time-honoured pair. It is through the rituals of feast that we demonstrate our communion in agreed and understood language. These accepted expressions of celebration help us give flesh to our most natural cravings: the cravings we share for belonging and community.

As humans, we know instinctively that we are more whole when we are together. We are naturally tribal. Just as in the creation story of Judaism God declares that 'it is not good that the man should be alone' (Genesis 2:18), we know instinctively that we are diminished in isolation. So we feast, and we feast together. We feast at the welcoming of a child; we feast at birthdays, graduations and promotions; we feast at betrothals and marriages and anniversaries; we feast when deals are made and new alliances formed. We feast to welcome, to farewell, to celebrate, to boast, to remember, to bond and to encourage. We even feast to mourn.

The old gold-fields town of Castlemaine in central Victoria is where I go to write. I stay in a bed-and-breakfast, always the same house, the same room. It's a simple space with a desk, a bay window and a view of the well-kept garden beyond. Often there are other guests about, though I go to write, not talk, and so avoid mingling wherever possible. To claim this as an act of discipline would be dishonest; my natural shyness makes solitude more preference than virtue. I have found breakfast the only hazardous point of the day, for one long dining room table means conversation is unavoidable if eating times collide. They did today.

An elderly couple, about the age of my own parents I suspect, was already fussing about the automated coffee machine when I arrived. With hot water streaming into the pan beneath, they looked almost frightened by the multiple buttons, pushing everything, all at once, but with no success. 'I can't stop it!' the woman kept saying, panic rising in her voice.

'Good morning,' I said as I walked in behind them, 'Can I help you?' I reached in past her shoulder and pushed the off-switch. 'That should do it,' I said.

'Oh glory be!' She looked more relieved than was really necessary.

'Can I do that for you?' I asked. 'Coffee?'

'Oh yes please, just a little milk,' said her husband, evidently shaken by this averted catastrophe.

'I can make my tea,' the woman said sheepishly, 'I have my hot water now.' She smiled without looking up.

The man immediately extended his hand, his face marked by the deep lines of age and hardship. 'I'm Reg, and this is Ellen,' he said, smiling warmly. As we settled down at the table there was a moment of silence as they stirred their cups.

'What brings you to Castlemaine?' I finally asked, 'Are you travelling?'

With that simple question, Reg unbottled. 'Our granddaughter was

The Festive Table

killed in a car accident on Saturday.' His eyes immediately filled with tears. 'She was only eighteen. We were on holidays in Queensland when our daughter called to tell us. We flew straight down.' His voice petered out.

'They live on a farm just out here in Newstead,' Ellen continued. 'We stayed with them for the first two nights, but they need their space.' Without looking up, Reg nodded while Ellen continued, 'It's all just too much. They're just in shock really.'

I listened, meeting their eyes whenever they looked my way. It was all I could do. 'I am so sorry,' I kept saying.

As they talked – something they clearly needed to do – I heard more of this young woman and her aspirations, her mother and father and siblings, and of plans for the funeral this coming weekend. I heard, too, that Reg had worked for forty years at the Melbourne Wholesale Fruit and Vegetable Market and that they had lived in the same house in Richmond for all that time. Despite his rugged, road-map complexion, Reg was clearly the more expressive one. His chin quivered as he ate his cereal, tears formed at the corners of his eyes as he sipped his coffee, and he quietly wept as he waited for his scrambled eggs to arrive.

By contrast, Ellen shed no tears. She only held her husband's hand and spoke softly of the pain she felt for her daughter. 'How do you go on?' she kept asking. This woman was clearly the working bee of the family, the one who for so long had kept everything together, managing, caring, hovering, doing. 'We'll go again today, just to do whatever we can,' she said.

We talked a little of what the day ahead would hold and of the little tasks that were required at a time like this. 'Will you cook?' I asked, though expecting the answer that came.

'Oh good heavens, no!' Ellen said with wide eyes, 'you should see the food. The benches are just covered with it.' She described in detail the unending arrival of gifts at the front door, all edible: casseroles, bread, cakes and scones, hams, boxes of fruit and eggs, and endless trays of lasagne. 'It just keeps coming!' Ellen was clearly overwhelmed by the love, overwhelmed by the volume, and just overwhelmed. 'It makes me remember when my father died,' she said, looking across at Reg. 'It was just the same. My poor mother with four daughters left alone, but the food, it came from everywhere ... just the same.'

Just as weddings are part of my 'trade', so too is death and the rituals that surround it. To sit with people in the initial stages of grief, to guide them as gently as one can through the planning of funerals and memorials is always a privilege, yet one of the most challenging things I do. Each occasion of loss is unique, every funeral service an experience of its own, but there is one thing I have noticed that flows from death to death: the food. In Ellen's words, it's just the same.

Why is the provision of food our most instinctive response to another's grief? Perhaps it's tied to our lack of words: when you don't know how to say it, cook it. Or is it that food is nurturing, the most natural expression of care? Perhaps, too, the gathering of food is our communal defiance of death and our claiming of life. Certainly, when we provide food, we affirm the role of the feast, even in death, as our most tangible expression of solidarity and togetherness.

Granted, food is an awkward thing at a wake. It seems almost crass to notice such a mundane provision, and yet without it there is no excuse to be together. It is both marginal and central at the same time. The Australian food writer Romy Ash reflects on this awkward role food plays in death. 'Is it a betrayal to eat ravenously as you mourn?' he asks. 'I would say that yes, in a way it is, but it is a necessary betrayal. We must eat to live.' Somehow in feasting together we hold death, we eat death and defy it; we claim life and gulp strength for the emptiness ahead.

While no funeral is easy, it's the funeral of a child that is most galling. Even for one accustomed to the rituals of death – one who has learned to be measured in response to grief and is generally able to find the right tone and appropriate words – I find 'measured' such an elusive thing when the deceased is a child, especially one I have known personally. Oliver was one of those, just two years old when his life tragically ended. He was a little boy who had struggled for life since his hazardous birth and though his parents had expected this day to come, the sadness of those who grieve a dead child fills a room with such heaviness it is hard to breathe. I will never forget the presence of Oliver's older sister in that room as the extended family gathered after the funeral: a small girl, five years old, moving about with a plate of cupcakes. They were little cakes she had made with her aunt, iced and decorated with brightly coloured smarties, green frogs (a favourite of Oliver's) and sprinklings of hundreds and thousands. As this little girl stood below me holding up her plate of cupcakes, offering a taste of her own sadness and delight mixed together in the fluorescent icing, I understood afresh how important food is when we mourn.

As well as an act of celebration or mourning, feasting is an expression of shared identity, history and nationhood. To feast together is to tell a common story and claim our belonging on a canvas much larger than that of an individual or a particular household. It says, 'We are who we are together.' Commonly, at the heart of such communal feasting lies an act of sacrifice.

As a fledgling nation, Ancient Israel understood itself through its feasts. Its defining moment in history was memorialised and made present in the Passover meal. To comprehend just how vital this meal was and is to Jewish identity, we have to understand its backstory. During a period of devastating drought and famine, the patriarch Jacob and his extended clan found refuge in Egypt. Three hundred years later, this familial tribe, now known as the Hebrews, was still there, having multiplied beyond all expectation. In fact, the Hebrews now outnumbered the powerful Egyptians. Pharaoh's response, motivated as much by fear as power, was first to enslave the Hebrews and second, to savagely cull their numbers. Year by year the level of oppression increased, moving from enslavement to appalling acts of genocide.

It's here that the ever-reluctant liberator Moses entered the picture. Divinely compelled, Moses became the mouthpiece of his God, calling upon Pharoah to let the Hebrew people go. From this point on, the story reads like an arm wrestle between Pharoah and Moses, with God coaching Moses from the sidelines. After the suffering of numerous nasty plagues – think locusts, frogs and rivers of blood – the stakes for Pharoah and his stubborn refusal to relent rose ever higher. The final plague, the game changer, was the awful slaughter of Egypt's first-born sons. On this particular dark and gruesome night, Moses directed the Hebrews to paint the blood of sacrificial lambs on their doorposts. If they did so, death's ominous curse would pass over them. And so it did. Faced with the horror of this curse's impact, a grieving Pharoah, mortified by the death of his own son, relented. Liberation was secured and the Hebrews went free.

The Book of Exodus, appropriately named, describes the feast of the Passover in painstaking detail, a feast to forever remember this nation-making event in Jewish history. In the first month of the year and on the tenth day, each household was to select a one-year-old lamb without defect and then slaughter it at twilight on the fourteenth day. Some of the blood was to be put on the side and top of the doorframe of the house. The meat was then roasted over a fire and eaten with bitter herbs and unleavened bread. The whole animal was to be eaten, and anything left over was burned. The people were directed to eat the meal in haste, with their cloaks tucked into their belts and sandaled feet and staffs at the ready. In the seven days following the Passover meal, known as the Feast of Unleavened Bread, no yeast was to be touched, kept in the house or eaten. The haste of liberation called.

These feasts, along with others that mark the Jewish calendar, serve as tangible reminders to the people of Israel of their nationhood and their self-understanding as the chosen people of God. Even today, it is in feasting that the Jewish people know who they are, where they came from, and where they are headed.

This connection between feasting and sacrifice can be found in ancient cultures the world over. The sacrifice might be an offering of thanksgiving to the heavens for the provisions of the harvest. It might be a sacrifice to appease an angry deity or a twisting of the earth's arm, securing blessing and prosperity for a community. For the Hebrews, sacrifice was a seal of relationship with their God. The command to burn the first fats of an animal was a ritual of invitation for God to come near. Whichever the case, what underlies all sacrificial acts is the assumption that only through death do we find life, only in surrender do we embrace something new. As Elizabeth Luard writes, this simple belief 'that a drop of blood shaken on the earth will bring forth good things' lies somewhere deep within the feast from east to west. While in many developed cultures acts of animal sacrifice are now abhorrent, there remains a persistent connection between feasting, identity and sacrifice.

We Australians love to feast, too, and through feasting we express who we are. Granted, our founding stories of white settlement in this land are not nearly so well defined as those of nations like Israel, nor does the notion of sacrifice sit easily in our celebrations. We more recent arrivals to this island continent might better identify with Egypt the oppressor than with the Hebrew slaves. Still, come Australia Day or other national days of celebration, there's nothing like a good barbecue to sedate our powers of reflection. It's amazing what the smell of a sausage and fried onions can do.

In 1934 my home city threw a feast to celebrate its centenary of founding. Melbourne's beginning is marked by a notorious deal struck between the unscrupulous John Batman and the local Duttigalla Aborigines. For a pitiful exchange of scissors, beads and blankets, and the promise of 'a yearly rent of similar kind', Batman 'purchased' six hundred thousand acres of land upon which this city is built.

The centenary feast was to be a barbecue of unprecedented scale. In her book *Bold Palates*, the food historian Barbara Santich tells the story in detail. Held at Laverton, the feast was to include an aerial pageant of RAAF warplanes, formation flying and dogfights, displays of bombing and parachuting, along with the usual mix of singing, dancing and fireworks.

With large crowds expected, plans were made to roast twenty bullocks over open fires, but when fifty thousand tickets sold within days of their release, more bullocks had to be found. Still, no one could have imagined the two hundred thousand people who showed up on the day nor the absolute chaos that ensued. While the worst of the Great Depression may have passed, the alluring aroma of a barbecue – a feast with an abundance of food and good cheer – was more than enough to whet the appetite of a city hungry for community, identity ... and meat.

Since then, our attraction to the communal feast has continued. From harvest picnics to racing carnivals, from our World's Longest Lunches to Australia Day barbecues, our attraction to feasting together remains strong, as does our longing for a shared sense of nationhood. It is the notion of sacrifice that is more problematic. In truth, our narratives of sacrifice are often conflicted. The blood spilt on this earth is more likely the blood of those we dispossessed than our own. Certainly we have known sacrifice, but as a national story it has been our blood shed on other lands that we remember most passionately. The spiritual attraction of the Anzac Day commemorations in places like Gallipoli only deepens with the passing of years.

Perhaps a genuine spirituality of the feast will only be ours as a nation when we more willingly embrace the stories of dispossession and sacrifice in this land as well as those in lands far away. Rather than allowing the aroma of the barbecue to distract us from this story, we might allow it to remind us of it: the good, the bad, the noble and the shameful. Any spiritual experience worth its salt will take us to the depths of confession before lifting us to the heights of celebration.

It's true, we've never been an overtly religious culture. As a secular society, one that has long maintained a boundary between state and religion, we've never had the intermingling of cultural and religious identity that shapes the feasting of others. Certainly the seasonal celebrations of Easter and Christmas define our year, though for us these have much more to do with the gathering of the clan than with notions of shared piety. That said, there remains a deep and profound spirituality in our country and one that I believe can be tapped most poignantly in the shared feast. But for this to be so, it must be an honest feast.

I will long remember one hot summer day a few years back, wandering along the banks of the Yarra River here in Melbourne. It was January 26, Australia Day, and Melburnians were out in force. Not far east of the

Princes Bridge, there were two large gatherings of people on opposite sides of the river. On one side, a large and boisterous group of young men and women with an Australian national flag draped from an overhanging branch and music blaring. On the other side was an equally large but more subdued group, people of all ages and ethnicities gathered under an Australian Aboriginal flag along with a banner that read 'January 26, Invasion Day'. What struck me more than anything was the fact that both groups were turning sausages on their barbecues.

As much as we have ever done, we gather today around barbecues and picnic rugs to lay some claim to who we are, and so we should. As it was in 1934, so it remains: we are drawn to the feast not just by the aroma of the chops; we come hungry for identity and community. How much richer that feast would be if it represented a coming together of stories from both sides of the river, an honest telling of a combined story that includes all Australians – from the most ancient to the most recent – and one that honours the sacrifices made. It's likely such a story will make us cringe as often as it makes us proud. But it will be our story and our feast. And as we tell it and retell it, we can light up the grill, pass the paper plates and lift our glasses. Here's to us!

As a young apprentice cook in a large hotel, I spent much of my brief tenure preparing feasts of various kinds; large, extravagant feasts for large, extravagant people. In the hotel's Grand Ballroom, and grand it was, our task was to impress with a stage set for culinary theatre. Glorious, illuminated ice sculptures would rise dramatically from centre stage with the most opulent displays of seafood, crushed ice and cascading champagne flowing down to the lavish buffet below. Beautiful *chaudfroid* meats, now out of style, were my specialty, as were rich desserts, intricate chocolate lace work, decadent creams and displays of the most gorgeous seasonal fruits you can imagine.

These feasts were arranged, most often, with very demanding 'hosts', those who were footing the substantial bill and were determined to impress. It has always been my experience in such contexts that the more one has, the more one bears a distinct sense of entitlement. Working routinely with such people, our banquet manager's masterfully balanced skill set of diplomacy, subservience and professionalism was constantly challenged. As the audience arrived for the feast, it was this 'host' who stood proudly in its midst, drawing greedily whatever credit and kudos flowed from their indebted guests while we cooks slinked discreetly away as though we had never been there.

While feasting is something we commonly do to celebrate, to mourn, and to claim our shared identity, feasting also has a long history as an act of indulgence and ego. History is littered with those who have used the feast to claim glory, exercise power, and enforce brutal but elegantly veneered systems of social exclusion. In his book *Feast: A History of Grand Eating*, historian of art and culture Roy Strong tells the fascinating story of feasting from the Greek symposium to the Victorian dinner party, from the Medieval feast to the grand banquets of the Renaissance and everything in between. What all these tables share in common are first, the chief end of glory to the king, pope, lord or master who hosts the feast, and second, the feast in all its guises as an index of social position, privilege and aspiration. Some things never change.

It is little wonder that when it comes to the language of virtue and vice, feasting sits obesely in the latter category while fasting, lean and haloed, stands virtuous in the opposite corner. The fact is, when feasting is synonymous with blatant excess and greedy displays of abundance, this common misconception flourishes, but misconception it is. It is not feasting that is fasting's opposite, but gluttony. Gluttony knows nothing of sacrifice or self-offering. Gluttony lives only to consume, to gather and hoard for itself. Feasting and fasting, on the other hand, are potentially two sides of the same virtuous coin, for when both have sacrifice at their core both have a capacity to enrich our lives in community.

It is only when feasting loses its connection to sacrifice, to self-giving and communion, that it loses its genius. Theologian Norman Wirzba argues that essential to good feasting in all its forms is a 'sacrificial sensibility'. Without it, feasting becomes vain, self-serving and ultimately destructive. With it, feasting becomes one of the 'correcting rhythms' of the good life, the life we live together. We do it at the wedding feast, the birthday party, the celebrations of graduations and promotions. We even do it at a funeral. We say in unison, life is grace and we live this grace together.

When feasting is nothing more than the self-glorifying display of the host, then it follows that the feast will have consumption at its heart. In a consumerist culture where conspicuous consumption is the mark of success and prestige, what is digested is never named as grace, but is only a sign of the host's power and wealth. The true feast is one through which we determine not to forget the grace and blessing of the world that is ours ... together.

◆ RECIPE

Lasagne for Sharing

In a beautiful essay on the place of food in mourning, Romy Ash tells the story of a friend who lost her mother. In the days immediately following the death, Romy says her friend was inundated with lasagne, 'dozens of them.'

> She had a freezer full. For weeks on end she ate different versions of minced meat, rich tomato sauce and bechamel, and now a lasagne, if she can face eating one, will always taste of sad.

What is it about lasagne? Easy to make? Easy to transport and share? Perhaps it's a comfort food, substantial and reassuring; sustaining and warming when the cold winds of grief and loss blow through. It may be that when we leave a tray of lasagne on the doorstep we leave a generous serve of our love and support when words are difficult. Regardless, a good lasagne is more than its layers of meat sauce, pasta and cheese. It means something. Even better, my children like it and eat it with relish. It's a stayer.

Ingredients
- Olive oil
- 1 large brown onion, diced
- 6 cloves of garlic, finely chopped
- 500 grams of minced pork or beef (or a mixture of the two)
- 3 tablespoons of tomato paste
- 4 tomatoes, peeled and chopped (or 1 can of chopped tomatoes)
- 2 cups of stock, preferably beef
- Salt and pepper
- 3 sprigs of thyme
- 4 sheets of fresh lasagne (cooked) or 1 packet of instant lasagne
- 350 grams of ricotta cheese
- 4 hard-boiled eggs
- Grated cheese, preferably a combination of mozzarella and parmesan

Method
- Preheat oven to 180°C.
- Heat the oil in a heavy-based saucepan or frypan.
- Add diced onion and sauté until soft.
- Add garlic and sauté a further minute or so.
- Add the minced meat and cook, stirring regularly with a wooden spoon until the meat crumbles and browns.
- Add the tomato paste and cook for a further few minutes.
- Add tomatoes, stock, salt, pepper and thyme, and bring the mixture to boil. Turn the heat down to a gentle simmer; cover and cook for thirty minutes.
- Remove cover and continue cooking for another twenty minutes, reducing the fluid so that the mixture is the consistency of a rich sauce. If the mixture becomes too dry, simply add some extra stock along the way.
- In an oblong baking tray (approximately 25cm across) lay one sheet of fresh lasagne (or equivalent in instant lasagne) to cover the bottom of the tray.
- Cover the lasagne sheet with a third of the meat sauce.
- Lay another sheet of lasagne, then spread two-thirds of the ricotta cheese on top and slice the eggs over the ricotta.
- Lay another sheet of lasagne on top, then cover it with half of the remaining meat sauce.
- Lay another sheet of lasagnae, then top with the remaining meat sauce.
- Dot the meat sauce with spoonfuls of the remaining ricotta and sprinkle over the grated cheese.
- Bake in the oven for about forty-five minutes.
- Serve with a fresh garden salad, some good crusty bread and a glass of something good. My beloved says red.

CHAPTER 8

The Multicultural Table
Eating, Culture and Inclusion

Boris Kiner is a Russian-Jew. He was born and raised in the Soviet state of Moldova. With the disintegration of the USSR, Moldova regained its political independence in 1992, but internal conflict was rife: ethnic Moldovians on one side and ethnic Russians on the other. Boris and his family, along with other Jews, were caught perilously in the middle, bearing the brunt of the insecurities and fears of people on both sides. With anti-Semitic feelings deepening, Boris' childhood memories of the Jewish ghettos and concentration camps resurfaced. The nightmares and flashbacks were terrifying; he was desperate to get his family out. With nothing but the clothes on their backs and one small carry bag of personal belongings, Boris and his family fled Moldova, never to return. Eventually they found a new home in Australia. Today Boris says he has no feelings for his home country and no desire to return, but in his kitchen he continues to cook *mamaliga*, a Moldovian dish of polenta. It is shared generously and eaten by the handful, dipped in butter and crumbled feta. Boris remembers it as 'a working man's food' for the long, cold days of the Russian winter. When he eats it today, he is comforted.

Dieu Pham is Vietnamese. Her husband was a colonel in the South Vietnamese army during the Vietnam War. When the North finally claimed victory, all the soldiers of the South were interned in 're-education camps'. At first Dieu Pham was told her husband would be gone for ten days, but he did not return. Weeks, then months passed and still no word. Years later, lower-ranking soldiers began returning home but not Dieu Pham's husband. Eventually she secured permission to visit him once every three months and did so faithfully for many years. Ten years to the day that her husband had been interned, Dieu Pham received a letter saying he would be released in fifteen days. She planned his homecoming meal with tears of relief and joy, a beautiful dish of *banh it*, special prawn and pork dumplings cooked only for the most important occasions. Now happily resettled in Melbourne, Dieu Pham still makes her special dumplings and still with tears of joy.

Mary is from Chile. She left her country in the late 1970s after the socialist president Allende and his government were overthrown by a military coup. The notorious General Pinochet took power and the early years of his new regime were marked by death and torture across the country. In fear for her life, Mary fled and found her way to Australia. Years later, when refugees were being airlifted out of El Salvador with nothing but the clothes they were wearing, Mary volunteered to help support one of the families as they resettled. The family assigned to her was living in a hostel and told her, once their friendship was secure, how much they craved the food from home. The only food they knew since arriving was the bland Australian fare served in a large impersonal dining room at the hostel. That day Mary took the family out and they searched the supermarkets high and low for the right beans and bought a camp stove. That night, in secret, on the floor of the single room the family shared, they cooked a meal of beans on their little stove. 'I'll never forget how good it tasted,' Mary said.

Sinh Khein is Vietnamese and remembers her years in a refugee camp in Singapore following the Vietnam War as she awaited acceptance into another country. She was one of just a small number accepted for resettlement in Switzerland. Held in Swiss detention for three months while her visa application was processed, Sinh Khein craved Vietnamese food and wept every night for her home and family. Upon her release into the community, the first thing Sinh Khein did was to make the long journey from Switzerland to France to buy the ingredients for spring rolls. It was a full day's journey to cross the border and return with the food she needed. Once back in her tiny apartment, she made a large platter of spring rolls and gave a party for her sponsors. Sinh Khein made this journey once a week for the eight years she lived in Switzerland. Finally she was reunited with her family here in Australia, where her spring rolls are still legendary.

These four stories are borrowed from a collection gathered by Melbourne's Immigration Museum in 2004 and published under the simple title *Cooking Stories* (edited by Julie Shiels). To prepare for the exhibition, representatives of refugee communities – including Timorese, Vietnamese, Chilean, El Salvadorian, Sri Lankan, Afghani, Russian Jews, Afar, Ethiopian and Iraqi – were invited around a table to cook for each other and to tell their stories of journey, arrival and settlement. The result is a potent illustration of the extraordinary role food plays in expressing who we are. Each story in the collection includes a recipe. Culture, identity and story are all bound together in Boris' sticky handfuls of polenta, in Dieu Pham's tear-stained dumplings, in Mary's secret beans, and in Sinh Khein's spring rolls. What's on the plate is who they are, where they come from, and what they most value. Their food is their story.

The anthropologists Farb and Armelagos say that the surest way of discovering a family's ethnic history is to 'look into its kitchen'. Long after dress, manners and speech have changed and become indistinguishable from the majority, old food habits continue as 'the last vestiges' of a family's culture of origin. The truth is, those vestiges last for generations. The strong aroma of tomato and garlic will still fill the kitchens of the descendents of Italian immigrants long after the passing of their ancestors, just as the distinctive tastes of fish sauce and chili will linger in the kitchens of those whose great grandparents fled to these shores from Vietnam. Taste and identity are infused.

The world's history of food is marked by three major empires, each distinguished by its staple: wheat, rice or maize. More particular separations of culture are found in what's added to these staples: olive oil in the Mediterranean, soya in China, chili in Mexico, butter in Europe, aromatic spices in India. And for my teenage son, tomato sauce. In his *Intimate History of Humanity*, the historian Theodore Zeldin tells the story of the Russian riots of 1840 when the government tried to persuade its people to grow potatoes. Accustomed as they were to the taste of rye bread, they suspected a plot to turn them into slaves or enforce a new religion. Fifty year later, however, they were in love with potatoes. According to Zeldin, their new love was found in what they added to their spuds. It was the same sourness – *kislotu* – that had long given a distinctive flavour to their food and to which they were addicted, both physiologically and culturally. 'Every people puts its own scent on its food,' says Zeldin. And it's a scent that lingers.

Like many other cities of the world, Melbourne's story – a story shared nationwide – is one of multiple cultures co-existing, melding and adapting. The scent of our tables is a pungent mix of stories and traditions. Today Australians celebrate a multicultural identity that has few peers in our global community. We claim this cultural diversity as evidence of an advanced, twenty-first century, cosmopolitan society, and justly so. Having welcomed nearly seven million people to our shores since the end of the world wars, we now speak more than two hundred and twenty languages in our homes. Nowhere is this diversity more evident than at our tables.

Long before the new settlers in this country arrived, Australia was already a richly diverse mix of cultures and menus. The indigenous peoples represented seven hundred different 'nations', spoke in excess of two hundred and fifty languages, and ate from more than five thousand different native food species across the continent and its adjoining islands. Traditional hunters and gatherers, these diverse tribes had learned to sustain themselves on what was immediately available. In the coastal north and the island communities, seafood played a key role in the diet, as did the gathering of fruits in the tropical north-east. In the arid central regions of the continent, plants, seeds and edible insects and grubs were part of the daily menu, along with eggs, bush fruits and nectars. Here in Victoria, home to the Kulin nation – a robust alliance

The Multicultural Table

of five different communities with distinct but related languages and customs – fishing and farming eels provided prime sources of protein, alongside other practices of hunting and gathering. Though the new arrivals to this land knew nothing of this complex and varied menu, it remains a foundational part of our table story.

The first new settlers who came in the 1800s were predominantly British, though others, less known, came from cultures far and wide and brought with them their own eating traditions. They included Chinese gold diggers, American sealers, farmers and vinedressers from Germany, camel herders from Afghanistan and Pakistan, Italian builders and artisans, and miners from Croatia. Statistics from the early 1900s have the French, Chinese and German all vying for second place after the British in the country's immigration stakes. The adapting and melding of these incoming stories and traditions added richly to the slow evolution of our table life. The food historians Jean-Louis Flandrin and Massimo Montanari call this the 'contamination' of culture, as essential as it is universal in the development of food traditions. The contamination continues.

Today the food landscape in Australia is extraordinary. What's on our plates is barely recognisable from what was there fifty years ago. From a relatively bland diet of meat-and-three-veg, typically overcooked, many of today's Australian households are feasting on a pantry-load of pulses, stir fries, curries, salads and breads unheard of in the past. Our infatuation with fowl has well and truly surpassed our love of red meat, and our passionate affair with seafood shows no sign of slowing. Once limited to the occasional poached cod with white sauce, we are now as familiar with salt-and-pepper squid and herb-encrusted salmon cutlets. What's more, we're now marinating and spicing with new abandon.

If we are not up for cooking ourselves, the take-home options have morphed from fish-and-chips wrapped in yesterday's newspaper or sweet-and-sour from the local Chinese take-away, to a veritable buffet of waxed boxes and plastic containers filled with whatever our bellies crave: there's pizza, gourmet burgers, fried chicken and tacos; there's Italian pastas, Vietnamese noodles, Chinese dumplings, Thai tom yum and a smorgasbord of fragrant Indian curries with a bag of naan bread to mop up the leftovers. Head out for dinner and the options are even more tantalising, from Argentinian to Ethiopian, Malaysian to Italian, Moroccan to Japanese, Spanish to French. And in many of the more creative and costly food halls there's a dizzying fusion of methods, ingredients and cuisines on the menu, sometimes all on the one plate.

There's no doubt, our food culture has been immeasurably enriched by the arrival of food traditions from other shores, and in our rediscovery of the food traditions that were already here. Our palates today are educated and extended, our appreciation for the rich cultural traditions of the world is deepened, and the cross-pollination of table stories knows a freedom unheard of in the past. Indeed, the culinary neighbourhood is so much smaller than it ever was before, and our multicultural table is well and truly set.

Of course, all is not perfect at this multi-coloured table of ours. The longer we sit the more we notice, or perhaps the more oblivious we become. The truth is, our tablecloth is stained. In fact, there are some things hidden under it that we've come to ignore. And the seating arrangements, once noticed, are awkwardly telling – who sits where and who's not there. It is the imperfections of Australia's multicultural table, unacknowledged and unaddressed, that ultimately diminish the celebration. And we are all the poorer for it.

Though the story of Australia's settlement is one of extraordinary diversity, it is hardly a warm and embracing tale. In the first instance, there is the diminishment, even eradication, of indigenous food cultures that were here and thriving when those first convict ships sailed into view. Captain James Cook, upon his earliest assessment of this new land as a place of settlement, famously concluded in 1770, 'The land naturally produces hardly anything fit for man to eat and the natives know nothing of cultivation.' It is only in the most recent years that we have begun to plumb the depths of the richness that Cook and others were never able to see – what was dismissed from, even lost, to our shared table, never to be regained. And then there is our shameful history of racism toward those of non-Anglo backgrounds who have arrived to help build the nation and enrich our culinary culture. The early Chinese prospectors who came in search of gold, often resorting to small-scale industries of market gardening and cooking, experienced a society unashamedly racist and unwelcoming to people 'of their kind'. And the Chinese were not alone. Many people of colours other than white and languages other than English found the Australian table a distinctly inhospitable one.

This racism became policy at the beginning of Federation in the passage of the Immigration Restriction Act (1901). This legislation marked the beginning of the White Australia Policy, a series of acts incorporated into Australia's immigration law privileging British migrants (and others of Anglo heritage) over all others. Arthur Calwell, Australia's first Minister for Immigration appointed in 1945 by Prime Minister Ben Chifley, represented well the prevailing feeling of white Australia in his notorious assertion to Parliament that 'two wongs don't make a white'. In Calwell's Australia, every non-English immigrant would be matched by at least ten British immigrants to maintain the nation's wellbeing.

Though the dismantling of these policies began after the end of the Second World War, the early waves of post-war European immigrants who came to our shores can still tell the most heart-rending stories of marginalisation. It was the Italians and Greeks who opened their cafés and produce markets in suburbs and country towns nationwide, offering anglicised versions of their home-style dishes to satisfy local palates. While eagerly devouring their souvlaki, pizza and bowls of spaghetti bolognese, we happily labelled them 'wogs' and sneered at their obvious differences. Though we tell ourselves today it was as much a term of endearment – like Aussies, Poms and Kiwis – it was at the time a clear designation of otherness and a barely veiled statement of denigration in our post-war suburbs and towns.

It was not until 1975 when the Whitlam government passed its Racial Discrimination Act that racially based selection criteria for immigration was finally buried. The Minister for Immigration of the day was the flamboyant Al Grassby, a Queenslander of Spanish and Irish decent who looked more like a suburban used-car salesman than a minister of the crown. He is remembered still for his loud plaid suits and floral ties, but more importantly as the father of Australia's new multiculturalism. Just a handful of years earlier (1969), then Minister for Immigration Billy Snedden had called, in no uncertain terms, for a strictly enforced monoculture. The message was clear: if you come to these shores, leave your differences (and your garlic) behind. In stark contrast, Grassby believed the future of a diverse and thriving population was to be found in a commitment to cultural integration, not assimilation. In his renowned speech of 1973 he spoke publically and passionately of his dream for an Australian society 'not merely tolerating the presence of difference, but viewing the core of Australian identity as embedded in the notion of diversity'. Grassby's vision took hold. As economic historian Peter Shergold writes:

> No longer was the central image that of a bubbling melting pot into which all newcomers were expected to plunge, emerging after sufficient cooking as well-done Australians. Rather, the watchword was integration, a concept which saw value in allowing Asian newcomers, like other ethnic groups, to preserve and disseminate their ethnic heritage within the value-system and social customs built by the tradition.

Since Grassby, Australia has maintained large-scale multi-ethnic immigration, and the general consensus is that ours has been one of the world's success stories in building a harmonious and constructive multicultural society. Regardless, the debate about levels of immigration, our response to refugees seeking asylum and the value of multiculturalism has continued with considerable heat. The rise of Pauline Hanson's One Nation party and the 2005 riots in Cronulla are still recent history. Our residual fear of difference is never far from the table's surface.

For all this cross-pollination of culinary cultures and the radical extension of our palates gastronomically and politically, the reality is that we still rarely sit down at the table together. The anthropologist Ghassan Hage has been a strident critic of the relationship between migrant and non-migrant at Australia's multicultural table and, more particularly, in its restaurants.

The common practice of the table, Hage argues, illustrates a persistent imbalance of power between the 'migrant' and the 'host'. While the urbane host, well travelled and with a ravenous appetite for world food and culture, soirees from feast to feast, from restaurant to restaurant, the ethnic cook in the kitchen is rarely noticed. His or her experience is forever marginal and subservient to the enrichment of the host's flourishing multicultural credentials. While the host exits the restaurant's front door comparing her fragrant Thai curry laksa with the sour taste of the Malaysian *asam* variety, the cook sits on a milk crate at the back door, smoking his cigarette and going nowhere. Our newfound interest in the culinary treasures of 'bush tucker' beautifully bottled on the shelves of specialty food stores does the very same thing: cultural tourism without the necessity of any significant relationship. The host's otherness is secure.

Perhaps, some would argue, Hage is too dismissive of what is good in the current richness of our table and I agree, but his critique should still be heard. To eat together is to be equal. To sit at the same table, eye-to-eye and fork-to-fork – or chopstick-to-chopstick – is to meet on common ground. The civil rights movement of the 1950s in the southern United States began as a dispute over the right of 'negroes' to eat at the same lunch counters as the whites. More than that, it was the right to sit there *with* the whites. To share food at the same table is a covenantal act. It always has been. In the Ancient Near East, the incubator of food culture, the sharing of food carried lifelong bonds of obligation for host and guest. Though our table customs today don't carry such tangible commitments, obligations remain, for food still has a covenantal power. The Bantu people of Southern Africa call it 'the clanship of porridge'. When we sit at the table together, we engage in an act of relational intimacy. We are forever connected in a particular way. The esteemed food writer M.F.K. Fisher says it well:

There is a communion of more than our bodies when bread is broken and wine drunk. It's like religion. If you have a glass of water and a crust of bread with someone and you really share it, it is much more than just bread and water. I really believe that. Breaking bread is a simile for sharing bread ... you cannot swallow if you are angry or hateful. You choke a bit ... it's all very betraying, how we eat.

Betraying indeed. Hage's point is made. When the current practices of the multicultural table do nothing but reinforce basic imbalances of power between migrant and host, we have work to do. No matter how we dress up the act of cooking today, no matter how much we swoon over the new celebrity of the professional kitchen, the overwhelming majority of cooks – those most commonly set apart by colour, language and religion – go unseen and unnoticed. What they provide is an act of service, and the cultural demarcation between kitchen and dining room, between cook and guest, remains clear.

If we are genuinely committed to celebrating Australia's multicultural table, then, to draw on Grassby's vision, our challenge is to embrace table life that does not merely tolerate the presence of difference (in the kitchen), but embraces it as a vital component of its daily, sit-down character. What that means in practice is developing a table life that goes beyond diversity in our menu choices to genuine and lasting diversity in our table companionship.

Granted, such a practice does not come easily. Some would say it goes against the natural grain of human interaction. Deeply tribal, we are naturally drawn to those most like us, and we are uncomfortable with, even suspicious of, those who are not. There are barriers that keep us apart: it may be colour or language, dress, body art, or social customs of interaction that are sufficiently different to make us unsure and on edge. Eating together is meant to be an act of relaxation and friendship after all, not hard, cross-cultural work. But without that work, are we destined to a multiculturalism bereft of any lasting or transformative depth? I think so, but to eat differently is a challenging call.

The Multicultural Table

Just a few minutes walk from my office, in a bland, featureless, circa-1960s arcade, there is a small Nepalese café tucked away in a corner. It's a simple place with a make-do decor of brightly coloured yellow and green walls, pink floor tiles and framed pictures of Nepalese sights hanging slightly skewed on the walls. It offers a minimalist menu, popular with international students from the nearby business school. For less than ten dollars I can buy a small, stainless-steel platter of chicken or pork *momo*, traditional Tibetan dumplings served with a cup of clear bone soup and an Indian relish on the side. A plastic cup of lemon tea makes a meal. Ashmi works at the front counter, a young Tibetan student of small build, intelligent and polite. Her long hair is always pulled tightly back and her glasses a good match for her direct and efficient manner. She smiles warmly over the counter when I walk in. I like to imagine she's genuinely pleased to see me, though that may be nothing more than the wishful assumption of a white, middle-aged man in a sea of much younger and more interesting South Asian faces.

I always take a book with me. A lunch break hidden in a book is an introvert's survival strategy, I've learned. I put my book down on the counter to take money from my wallet. Predictably, Ashmi will lean over and read the title out loud: *'Old Worlds and New Australia'*, *'Sociology on the Menu'*, *'A Cook's Life'*. Most often she looks up and simply smiles. 'It's good!' I might say. Occasionally she will ask a question, most often about the meaning of a word in the title.

One lunchtime as I approached the counter, Ashmi pulled a small, carefully folded slip of paper out of her pocket, as though she had prepared for my arrival. Unfolding the paper and placing it on the counter, she asked, 'What does this mean?' I looked down to see the word 'dismiss' written in carefully spaced, lower-case letters.

I thought for a moment. 'To send away,' I suggested. 'At the end of a class, the teacher will dismiss her students. It's time for them to leave.'

'Ah, yes!' Ashmi wrote something with her pencil, then refolded the paper and returned it to her pocket. She smiled, took my money and the transaction was complete.

One afternoon my book was David Nichol's *The Bogan Delusion*. I placed it on the counter. 'Bogan,' Ashmi said, with a smile of recognition. 'What is this bogan?' she asked.

'You've heard it before?'

She nodded, smiling again.

'What do you think it means?' I asked.

'Oh, um, working-class, aggressive?' she suggested.

'You've met people like this?' I ask.

'Yes, sometimes people like this, they come here and I feel nervous.'

It's a good read, this bogan book, though our relationship did not begin well. In an early chapter Nichols asserts that Dandenong, the suburb of my childhood, has been voted one of the two most bogan places in Victoria; Moe comes second. Struggling to embrace my own bogandom, I almost put the book aside before being reassured by Nichols' argument, well made, that a term like bogan in our society is close to meaningless. Thrown around ad nauseam, especially in popular media, it's become one of those words that soaks up whatever prejudice we bring to it: John Howard's McMansion-loving aspirationals? Football-obsessed rednecks? Flag-waving boofheads with obnoxious tattoos? Or outer-suburban dickheads with their Commodores and trakkie daks? Who knows? What is consistent is the term's designation of 'otherness'. Bogans are those people out 'there' who are not like 'us'.

My own prejudice was brought home recently when a young man asked to meet me in a city café on Swanston Street. I had reconnected with him through a youth program working with an ad-hoc community of kids who gather on the steps under the clocks of the city's iconic Flinders Street Station. I knew Cody when he was just a small boy living with his mum in assisted housing in the outer suburb of Cranbourne. Now in his early twenties and disconnected from his family, he's living in a St Kilda boarding house and struggling to keep life together. We met in his café of choice on Swanston Street. It was one of those places with booths and a distinctly stale smell in the air; Chiko rolls, potato cakes and limp slices of pizza steaming behind glass; and a familiar menu of burgers, souvlaki and milkshakes that never changes. Cody ordered a burger and me a coffee. He ate and I drank. We talked. To begin I was uncomfortable, out of place and resistant. I looked suspiciously at the coffee sitting like dishwater in my cup. This was the café of my childhood. Then I knew nothing else; now, I cringed. I'll be honest; I felt superior and displaced. It wasn't being with Cody. It was being with Cody here.

The eating landscape of the city, even from one part of the street to the next, is a divided one. Most commonly we eat with those who are like us. To do otherwise feels awkward, uncomfortable. Ashmi is 'Asian', Cody 'bogan' and me, who knows? We each inhabit our own cultures, our own worlds and so we rarely sit together.

Like all cities its size, central Melbourne is home to a thriving university culture. Two of its largest, the University of Melbourne and RMIT University, have eighty thousand students between them, twenty-five percent of whom enrol from overseas. At points these two sprawling campuses intermingle, while the thoroughfare that runs between, the northern end of Swanston Street, is a densely packed strip of purpose-built student-housing high-rises, home to approximately ten thousand students, the vast majority from South-east Asia.

The University of Melbourne's own research shows that our integration of these students into the life of the city is pitiful at best. Exiting students will routinely testify to the fact they have never once entered the home of an Australian family, nor even shared a meal with an Australian citizen. Many remain in Australia after graduation, but the cultural divides already in place are stark and difficult to overcome. Ashmi is one of those international students. Occasionally, when I have come into the café in the late afternoon when there are very few customers, Ashmi will stand at the table and we'll talk, but I am conscious that I am an older man and a customer. I proceed tentatively. On two occasions now, I have taken another friend with me, a young Japanese woman I know from my teaching days. Mai is a very gentle woman, but outgoing and warm. As I expected, Mai has connected with Ashmi in ways I cannot. In fact, they have become friends. To my surprise, I came across the two of them seated in another café recently, a small Japanese-inspired tea house that I have passed by curiously many times.

It was odd meeting Ashmi outside of our usual context, and I could tell it was awkward for her too, but before long I was seated with them sharing tea and a gorgeous selection of house-made Japanese pastries, Mai's expert choice. Away from the divisions of the counter and the transactions of guest and host, we connected in ways I could not have planned. Ashmi spoke openly of her struggles with study, her family and her homesickness, and the funny things she had observed about Australian culture and food. We laughed and talked, sometimes struggling with language but more often delighting in this new connection. It was one of the most rewarding table encounters I have had for a long time, all made possible by the lubricant of tea and the equality of a shared table.

In his compelling book *Don't Go Back to Where You Came From*, academic and columnist with *The Age* Tim Soutphommasane offers a measured and convincing assessment of multiculturalism as one of our nation's great achievements, distinctive in important ways from that of other places. The ongoing challenge for our society, according to Soutphommasane, is negotiating the extraordinary cultural diversity that is ours as a result. As recent debates and tensions attest, it is a negotiation that is never entirely settled but is intimately entwined with issues of social justice, inclusion and equity. It is because of this that the value of multiculturalism cannot be diminished in our conversations about national identity and development.

For me, Soutphommasane's most challenging words are reserved not for those who oppose multiculturalism but for those who support it. It is too easy, he says, for supporters to rest their case on the 'ornamental' qualities of cultural diversity, most commonly ethnic foods and cuisines and the cosmopolitan lifestyles they enable. The result is nothing more than 'a lifestyle approach' to multiculturalism, painfully superficial and too easily dismissed by its detractors.

> Focussing on lifestyle can mean that we fail to recognize the civic dimensions of diversity. We can lose sight of how diversity demands of us answers not only about culture, but about justice and citizenship.

While Soutphommasane's call is to a deeper and more transformative multiculturalism, both civic and cultural – one that enables genuine inclusion, opportunity and participation for all who call this nation home – I suggest the answer is not to step away from the table as an 'ornament' of diversity, but to engage more intentionally with it as the central venue for real and lasting change.

Food, identity and story are so intimately entwined. A genuinely inclusive society is one in which every story is equally valued and can become part of the larger story that we live and tell together. This storytelling begins and continues at the table, a table defined not by the roles of guest and host but by the genuine equality of its relationships. It's a table where Boris, Dieu Pham, Mary and Sinh Khein can tell and claim their stories, their full stories, as part of their identity as citizens of this land. It's a place to serve and be served, to feed and be fed, to talk and to listen as equals. For this to happen we have to sit down together. It has always been the case that the shared table turns strangers into friends. Otherness evaporates over dinner. While the stranger may take our order, cook our food, and wash our dishes, never to be heard, known or understood, once they sit down with us to share both food and story, the transformations of friendship begin.

◆ RECIPE

Sinh Khein's Spring Rolls

In her family, Sinh Khein's spring rolls are legendary, an expression of their culture of origin and part of Sinh Khein's refugee story. Today spring rolls are ubiquitous in restaurants of all Asian varieties. Anglo-Australians have embraced them with gusto. Sadly, the more generic they become, the more we adjust to tasteless and poor-quality varieties, straight from freezer to deep fryer to our plates. But when you have tasted high-quality spring rolls made with fresh ingredients and care, the difference is stark. Making them yourself takes practice. As simple as it seems, the skills required take time to develop. But believe me, it's worth the effort.

Ingredients

Spring rolls
- 50 grams of dried wood ear (black fungus) mushrooms
- 50 grams of dried vermicelli noodles
- 500 grams of minced pork or chicken
- 1 brown onion, finely diced
- 2 carrots, grated
- 2 cm piece of fresh ginger, finely grated
- 2 cloves of garlic, crushed
- Approximately 30 sheets of frozen spring roll pastry
- Vegetable oil for deep frying

Dipping sauce
- 1 fresh red chili
- 1 teaspoon of sugar
- 3 tablespoons of fish sauce
- 4 tablespoons of water
- 2 tablespoons of julienne carrot (small matchsticks)

Method
- Set out the pastry to defrost.
- Soak the mushrooms in warm water for one hour. Drain and cut them into thin strips.
- Combine all the ingredients for the dipping sauce in a small bowl, cover and set it aside.
- Fill a wok or large saucepan two-thirds full of oil ready for frying.
- Soak the noodles in warm water for ten minutes. Drain and chop them into small pieces.
- Along with the mushrooms and noodles, mix together the grated carrot, diced onion, ginger, garlic and meat. Combine the mixture well by hand.
- Now for the fun part. Lay one spring roll wrapper onto a flat surface with the bottom corner pointing toward you. Place a heaped tablespoonful of the meat mixture close to the bottom corner of the wrapper. Brush the edges of the pastry lightly with water. Fold the bottom corner up and over the filling. From there, roll the mixture up firmly, folding the right and left edges in once you are about half way. Press to seal and place the completed roll onto a tray. Repeat with remaining mixture and wrappers.
- Cover the rolls with plastic wrap and refrigerate them until you are ready to fry. Sinh Khein puts hers in the freezer for a couple of hours.
- Heat the oil over medium-high heat until it's ready for frying. A good test is to drop a small piece of bread into the oil. If it sizzles immediately, the oil is ready.
- Fry the spring rolls in batches of three or four at a time. They usually take three to four minutes until they are golden brown. Transfer to a wire rack with a slotted spoon to drain and cool just a little.
- Serve with the dipping sauce and a serviette close by. They won't last long.
- Here's to you, Sinh Khein!

CHAPTER 9

The Communion Table
Eating, Sacrament and Connection

It is a handsome piece of furniture; cumbersome and ornate – personally, a bit too Franco Cozzo for my tastes – but beautiful just the same. Constructed from Victorian Blackwood, this grand ecclesial table sits front and centre in the one-hundred-and-sixty-eight-year-old sanctuary of Melbourne's Baptist church on Collins Street. Since the settlement's first Baptist service in 1836 when a congregation of sixty people gathered in a tent on the site of the Regent Theatre, a communion table like this one has been central to the church's life.

Today, sitting beneath the sanctuary's equally ornate pulpit, the table is flanked by five matching chairs, one centred behind it and standing throne-like as though its inhabitant might have a more notable place in heaven. Its eight solid legs, each one a thickly squared pillar of substance, give the table a sense of solidity and strength. Intricately carved wooden filigree of vines and wheat strands adorn their upper portions and span the open spaces between them. Together they provide an apron to the solid layer of polished wood that forms its top. Purpose-built for the sacred elements of wine and bread, the symbolism of grape and grain make the table's purpose clear. On its top rests a plain silver goblet, a simple but dignified symbol of sacrifice and one that catches the light filtering through the sanctuary's stained-glass windows.

If you get close enough – crouch down and squint if you need to – you'll see a small gold plaque just a few centimetres in width attached to the table's bottom rung. It reads 'In Memoriam, William Gardiner Sprigg, 19th July 1926.' Not surprisingly, Sprigg was a devout Baptist, committed member at Collins Street and lay preacher of formidable reputation. He was also Company Secretary for Melbourne Tramways Ltd, an astute and respected man of business who fared particularly well in his stockmarket speculations. At his death he left behind a stately East Melbourne address and a fortune of more than £100,000. With a desire to honour a good and devout man, Sprigg's family commissioned the construction of this table, calling upon the services of the esteemed Goldman furniture company in South Yarra and its chief designer Mr Treede. The finished product was presented to the church in 1927 on the occasion of its eighty-fifth anniversary. What was there before it for those eighty-five years I do not know. Regardless, here this one sits today, a holder of tradition and ritual beyond its own life.

Four years ago I was asked to consider taking up the appointment of minister of this old church. Re-entering the ministry was not in my career plan. Though deeply committed to the faith of the church, I was happily teaching in a tertiary institution and was content to do so for the rest of my working days, but the invitation was persistent. I knew the church. Most good Baptists do. The oldest continuing Baptist congregation in the nation, Collins Street has played a significant role in the life of our tradition and still stands at the centre of the city, as close to a cathedral as Baptist ecclesiology will allow. Its architecture is distinctive, pared back compared to other churches of similar age, simple in its design and with the table at its centre. In large part, it was this table that clinched the deal.

Before saying yes to the invitation, I stood alone in the sanctuary wondering just what good sense could bring me here. Old city churches come with as many layers of the immovable and unchangeable as they do with potential and opportunity. However, as I ran my hand over the surface of that old table and looked out across the sanctuary, its wooden pews fanning outward in symmetrical form, I had a sense that this was right. Here was a community of faith in the heart of one of the nation's great cities that understood itself and its purpose in light of this table.

The Communion Table

I have always understood the communion table as central to the church's identity. It is the table of Jesus, the one in whom Christians like me place their faith. Jesus was a man of the table, not just the one he shared with his disciples with offerings of bread and wine, but the multiple tables of daily life. How he lived and ate at these tables was a profound demonstration of the 'good news' he embodied and a call for his followers to do likewise.

I understand that the table of the Christian church, whatever brand, is not a table at which everyone feels comfortable. For myriad reasons it may be a table associated with beliefs hard to swallow or past experiences that have hurt or excluded. My purpose here is neither to win you over nor ask you to be seated at a table you cannot believe in. Rather, I want to illustrate an important point, one central to the subject of this book. To speak of a spirituality of the meal table is to speak of a way of sitting at the table that seeks connection to every aspect of our lives and integration with our most deeply held values. A life-giving spirituality of the table flourishes best when my life at one table is connected with my life at all tables, and when the way I sit at each table flows out of my deepest commitments, whatever they be. At its best, that's what the table of the church embodies and demonstrates.

Just days prior to his execution, Jesus gathered his followers together in a secluded, upstairs room and shared with them a final meal, a last supper. It was a celebration of the Passover and followed closely the traditions of this sacred Jewish feast. Leonardo da Vinci's portrayal of the night (and the endless parodies of it) has lodged this last supper in our memories – even the memories of those who have no particular investment in the story. Based on the account of the meal in John's Gospel, da Vinci's painting has Jesus, serene and especially well groomed, at the centre of a long table with twelve followers, all men, fanned out six on either side. Of course, da Vinci is painting in the fifteenth century. While he captures well the consternation of the disciples at the news that one of them will betray Jesus, just what da Vinci's glorious imagery has to do with the reality of the meal that night is anyone's guess. What is true is that this meal has so captured the Christian imagination that efforts to express it in art, music, poetry and liturgical tradition have consumed us for centuries. Leonardo was certainly not the first to put his paintbrush to the wall in its honour, nor would he be the last.

Indeed, this was a meal of high drama and profound significance. Jesus' reinterpretation of the Passover feast to reflect his own imminent sacrifice means that this meal has become the defining sacrament of the Christian faith. Jesus' words as he cradled both bread and wine, 'This is my body' and 'this is the new covenant in my blood', along with his exhortation 'do this in remembrance of me', have become the sacramental words of the church. Whatever we call it – Mass, Holy Communion, the Lord's Supper, the Eucharist, the Breaking of Bread, the Divine Liturgy – it describes a ritual as precious to the Christian community as any other, 'the signature dish of our faith' as the poet Milton Brasher-Cunningham describes it. What is delightful, or confounding depending on your perspective, is that this signature sacrament is a ritual of the dinner table, an act of eating and drinking. While the communion table today may be ornate and altar-like, exquisitely carved, surrounded by icons and stained glass, and set high in sanctuary or cathedral, it remains a table upon which dinner is served.

It also remains a table connected to every other table of life. For Jesus, this was not the only table at which he sat, nor was it the only table at which he participated in life-changing encounters or proclaimed eternal connections between earth and heaven. All through the gospel story, from the very earliest days of his public ministry to the last, Jesus is eating and drinking, so much so his detractors label him 'a glutton and a drunkard'. In his commentary on Luke's gospel, the New Testament scholar Robert Karris observes 'the aroma of food' issuing forth 'from each and every chapter'. Indeed, all through the gospel, page after page, Luke has Jesus going to or coming from a meal, sharing a meal, or telling stories about meals. The truth is, the aroma of Jesus' table behaviour gets up the noses of his enemies more than anything else he does. In fact,

Karris makes the controversial claim that 'Jesus got himself crucified by the way that he ate'. It's a proposition worth considering.

Jesus lived amidst the overlap of two cultures, both of which took the rituals of eating very seriously. In Greco-Roman culture you were defined socially by the company you kept at the table. Meal table etiquette was one of the most important expressions of social identity, order and stability. Everyday meals were highly complex events through which cultural values, boundaries, statuses and hierarchies were maintained. To uphold this order, one ate exclusively with one's own social or professional class – no exceptions. In an age when reciprocity was one of the building blocks of social organisation, an invitation to dinner meant an obligation to return the favour in equal kind. In an honour- and shame-based society, the inability to reciprocate in equal measure was devastating. Further, within one's class, strict seating regulations at the meal table demonstrated who fitted where in the social pecking order. Anyone who challenged these customs in Greco-Roman society was judged to be acting dishonourably; at worst, an enemy of social and political stability. The message was clear – don't rock the boat!

Things were much the same in Jewish society; where and with whom one ate was a matter of great importance, though for more religiously inspired reasons. At the time of Jesus, Jewish table practice was deeply tied to notions of religious purity. Following the destruction of the Jewish temple in 586 BC, there was a need to consecrate a new holy place for the presence of God. As one response, a group of devout people took it upon themselves to organise and keep their own homes as pure as the temple had been. By the time Jesus entered the picture, it was the Pharisees who were promoting this concept of the home as holy place. With a passion for national and personal righteousness, the Pharisees adhered to a complex set of home-based, dinnertime regulations through which racial and religious purity could be assured. In this particular expression of Jewish culture, the ritual purity of your dinner guests was as important as your own. It was in the sharing of food, given its cultural and covenantal importance, that one was most vulnerable to 'contamination'. To add to this table anxiety, complex purity lists were developed identifying up to sixteen levels of religious purity. Men like the Pharisees – priests, Levites and full-blooded Israelite males – were unsurprisingly at the top of the list, while at the bottom were those with physical deformities – the lame, the crippled, the blind. Non-Jews and those 'half-breed' Samaritans did not even make the list.

So, from one perspective an exclusive dinner table is the keeper of social stability, and from another, the keeper of religious purity. The table is clearly marked. It's into this context that Jesus walked and broke every rule in the ancient book of etiquette. The fact is, Jesus ate *anywhere* and with *anyone*. With no deference to status, profession, moral standing, family background, religious affiliation, race or gender, Jesus shared a meal with anyone who would have him, and invited still others along for the party. Was Jesus just a rebel, an ill-mannered bohemian or an awkward social misfit blissfully unaware of his numerous social gaffes? Clearly not. Jesus knew exactly what he was doing. According to Jesuit biblical scholar Jerome Neyrey, Jesus' selection of table companions was 'no mere lapse of regard' for traditional customs, but a carefully chosen strategy. Though tradition was clear that 'likes should eat with likes', Jesus' choice to eat with outcasts, sinners and foreigners was a formal signal that God's table was a confrontingly different one.

Jesus' critics were certainly riled. As the self-appointed gatekeepers of the table's exclusivity, they made no secret of their disgust. 'Look who he's eating with: tax collectors and sinners!' they fumed. 'Do you know what you are doing? Don't you know who these people are?' they demanded of him. Time and again Jesus' critics left these meals exasperated, angry and, most of all, fearful of Jesus' influence. So much so they began plotting his demise.

It's little wonder they wanted him gone. Through the simple act of eating, Jesus was challenging some of the most fundamental principles of order and exclusion that governed society. For Jesus, his point was a non-negotiable one, for life at the dinner table was a powerful metaphor for the table of God. Let it be known, Jesus was saying, that the invitation to God's table is open to anyone who will respond. All are welcome, regardless of race, social position, bank balance, religious background, colour, gender or sexuality. Through his dinnertime stories, Jesus described God's table as a great banquet to which God as host invites the cultural outsiders – the poor, the despised and marginalised, the blind and the lame – the very ones barred from most dinner tables in his day. Indeed, according to Jesus, it is the cultural elite and spiritually arrogant who are in danger of exclusion.

These radical proclamations of Jesus did not come out of thin air. Jesus was simply ushering in the order of God anticipated in the prophetic tradition of Israel. The prophet Isaiah had long anticipated a day when all boundaries and exclusions would be eradicated in favour of an inclusive table of redemption and liberation:

> On this mountain the LORD of hosts will make for all peoples a feast of rich food, a feast of well-matured wines, of rich food filled with marrow, of well-matured wines strained and clear. And he will destroy on this mountain the shroud that is cast over all peoples, the sheet that is spread over all nations; he will swallow up death forever ... the LORD has spoken (Isaiah 25:6–8).

As a young boy sitting restlessly in the suburban church of my childhood, I had little consciousness of the communion table as such a radical place. Truthfully, I dreaded communion Sunday. We Baptists don't set the church's table every week; usually it's once a month. Still, in my early judgment, this monthly ritual tacked on to the end of an already-long service simply shunted the 'just bearable' into the grey yards of Sunday morning despair. I would sink in my seat, shoulders slumped, watching the elusive prospect of lunch disappear over the horizon. Regardless, in that moment when the pastor held aloft the cup and spoke the words of Jesus, 'Remember me!' I would look up from my fog (and the comic book hidden in my hymnal) with a sense that something important was happening. I noticed at this point that my mother beside me always closed her eyes. I assumed this to be the posture for remembering and followed suit, sitting to attention and clenching my eyes as tightly as I could. It was a challenging task for a young boy, this remembering Jesus, given I had never met him in person. I imagined it to be akin to remembering my two grandmothers, both of whom died long before I was born. Still I did my best, recalling a picture of Jesus from my Children's Bible. He was a nice-looking man, tall, with flowing brown hair, neatly trimmed beard, gentle hands and dressed in a long white robe. I liked him, though his one-dimensional elegance made any sense of connection unlikely.

The challenge of picturing Jesus has never eased. Though intrigued by the myriad ways people and communities have rendered Jesus in visible forms, I have never found one to own. Regardless, this invitation to remember Jesus resonates more and more. The Catholic theologian Patrick McCormick calls the Eucharist 'a feast of remembering', but a remembering that is about much more than a family snapshot or the recollection of a particular moment, no matter how significant. For McCormick, it is a remembering of all that Jesus' life and death embodied. For this reason it's a dangerous remembering, an 'anamnesis' that opens us up to 'the dangerous memories of a Christ who stands with, embraces, and becomes one of the poor – who takes on the mortal and frail flesh of the hungry, the sick, naked, homeless, disposed, and disappeared'.

These dangerous memories include so much more than what happened in that upper room with the disciples the night before his execution, and even more than the sight of Jesus hanging on a cross. In this ritual of communion we are called to remember the one anointed to bring good news to the poor, release to the captives, healing to the sick and liberty to the oppressed; the one who took the form of a slave, gave up his own life for the sake of others and calls us to do the same; the one who said that when we forget the hungry, the imprisoned, the homeless and the sick, we forget him. 'Injustice begins with forgetting', McCormick says. The call of the church's table is a call to remember.

For many people like me, the sacrament of the table is a deeply personal one and rightly so, but in claiming it as personal we cannot make it private, secluded from the rest of life. It cannot be. While the rituals of communion may be celebrated in sacred buildings set apart from others, the table of the church can never be cloistered, unsullied by the rest of life. Certainly it is a table of extraordinary and personal grace, but the table of the church is about so much more than churchgoers feeling spiritually cosseted. Remembering Jesus means never forgetting the community of which we are a part. The table of Jesus is one that compels, obligates and sends — for it is connected to every table at which Jesus sat and to every table at which we sit today. Its holiness is found not in its seclusion and separation but in its connection.

If there is a standard-issue look for corporate executives, David has it. Tall and lean, sporting a pair of silver-rimmed glasses, and his short-back-and-sides flecked with the perfect ratio of grey; just enough to look distinguished but not out of date. We were seated together at a breakfast for business and community leaders in the Docklands. The floor to ceiling windows framed an uninterrupted view of the harbour and its marina full of luxury yachts rocking gently on the water below. I arrived late; the formalities had already begun. David smiled and nodded his welcome as I took my seat.

While I was glad of the smile, I immediately assumed some things about this man. We had never met before but I had him tagged. When a break came in the program, we turned to our places for breakfast and David introduced himself. His handshake was warm. I learned he was head of risk assessment for one of the city's leading financial institutions and I wasn't surprised. When it came to my turn I took a deep breath before explaining that I was a Baptist minister. I have learned that my vocational confession often comes with a cost. Raised eyebrows and a brief 'Oh!' is common before a rapid change of subject or seat. David was not fazed. 'On Collins Street?' he asked.

'Yes, that's right,' I said, relieved.

'I've heard about your work with the homeless,' he said, 'You have quite a reputation.'

I smiled, glad for an unusual moment of recognition.

As the conversation continued, David explained that he was raised and educated in the Anglican Church, though today he is unsure about what he believes and finds very little in the church to connect with. 'I suppose I'm still a cultural Anglican,' he said, 'but probably I'm more a doubter than a believer.' After chatting at length about our common struggles with faith, I asked David how he heard of the Baptist church. 'Oh,' he said with a smile, 'through an old friend of mine. His name was Gus. He's gone now, but he used to eat at your church café every now and then and talked about it.' David went on to explain that he had met Gus while sitting on a bench seat by the Yarra River. He had gone there to eat his sandwiches one lunchtime and Gus, sharing the seat, struck up a conversation: 'I was awkward at first. He was clearly homeless and obviously hadn't showered for a while, but I couldn't help but like him. It turns out we were about the same age, but from very different backgrounds. He was living on the street and I had a home in Hawthorn. He had no one and I had this whole extended family.'

Such was the connection that David felt with Gus that he returned to the same bench seat the next week in the chance that he would see him again. He did and so a tradition began: 'I'd bring a few extra sandwiches and a vanilla slice. He loved vanilla slices ... and chocolate Big Ms. We didn't talk about anything very serious, mainly the football. Occasionally he would tell me a bit about himself, but never in detail. He would always have a joke to tell me though. He was pretty funny!' David explained that what began as an ad-hoc thing developed for him into a commitment: 'Gus didn't always show up, but he was there most weeks and gradually it seemed to become as important to him as it was to me.'

I asked him why.

'For me? It became this really grounding thing,' David said, 'I spend most of my lunch times with people from the banks and government, the high flyers. I eat in places like this almost every day, with the views and the wine. After a while it skews your view of things. Sitting with Gus was this completely different experience. After a while I realised how much I needed it. I had my PA mark out every Wednesday lunch in the

The Communion Table

diary. I think she assumed Gus was a client or something. I never told her otherwise. We did it for nearly two years.'

David went on to tell me that Gus had passed away the year before: 'After a few weeks of him not showing up I was worried. I called around some of the social service agencies. All I had was his first name and I didn't even know if that was really it. But I finally found out that he had died of a heart attack at one of the rooming houses. I was devastated. I had not been able to go to a funeral or anything. He was just gone ... it was over.' 'He changed me though,' David continued. 'There was something about eating our sandwiches together that shifted things for me. I guess it was that Anglican education, that ethic that was drummed into us at school: love your neighbour as you love yourself. Gus made that real again.'

The encouragement of the communion table is not only for those who sit regularly in church. There is a principle in it for all of us, whatever religious brand we may or may not bear. The spirituality of the table is in its connection. Who we are at one table is connected to who we are at another. The values we hold in life find expression in our daily routines of the table, be it in the family home, in the neighbourhood café, or on the park bench with sandwiches and vanilla slice.

The church café that Gus frequented is called Credo. It's tucked away at the back of our buildings. The nondescript entrance is on Baptist Place, a narrow laneway that runs off Little Collins and ends at the church's backdoor. Heavily graffitied, Baptist Place has had a chequered history, a place that's been home to the darker side of the city's drug dealing and abuse. During the heroin epidemic of the early 1990s, overdoses on the church's back doorstep were commonplace. Paramedics grew accustomed to the unique challenges of access while church staff quickly developed skills of care they had never needed before. Out of this sense of 'crisis' for the church came the slow development of Credo, a place of welcome, nutritious food, basic support services and, most importantly, relationship. Almost two decades later and Credo remains the central focus of Urban Seed, a much broader community of service and hospitality to the city's most marginalised communities.

Still in the church's basement space, Credo is not your typical café. More homely than urban chic, there's a musty feel to the air as you enter and a laid back welcome for the odd collection of people who wander in and out. At one end of the space is an open kitchen and at the other a small raised platform with padded bench seats and shelves for books, candles and other odds and ends. Running down the centre of the main floor is a long communal table with smaller tables and chairs along the edges. It's a place where people from the streets come daily for a hot meal and company. Some live with serious substance abuse problems or struggle with mental illness. Many are homeless and unemployed; some come alone and others in groups. There are a few who arrive with children in their care. Some are hungry for conversation and others prefer solitude. It's table service at Credo; not a soup kitchen where people cue for their food, but one in which they're invited to sit and be waited on by those who volunteer their time to cook, serve, clean and hang out. The truth is there are many people who will come to the backdoor of the church and sit at the Credo table who will never grace the inside of the church's sanctuary nor sit at its communion table. Regardless, these tables are connected, each one an expression of the same commitments and the same community.

More recently, the church has established another café at its front door. In contrast to its back door, the church's front entrance is grand. Flanked by four white Corinthian columns, it's an entrance that suits the church's location at the 'Paris end' of one of Melbourne's premier streets. The Verandah Café, as it's known, could not be more different to Credo. Looking out over Chanel and Ralph Lauren stores, the Athenaeum Club to one side and the beautiful Georges building on the other, the Verandah Café serves lattes, short blacks and Phillippa's pastries. It's a place where office workers, neighbours and tourists drop by and sit for a while under the church's grand portico or shaded by the overhanging plane trees that line the Collins Street sidewalk. With its sun umbrellas and garden boxes, the Verandah Café provides a place for conversation, friendship and the slow nurture of neighbourhood. It welcomes people into the church's space without the obligations of belief or the intrusions of unwanted intimacy. Most of those who sit comfortably here will never come for a Sunday service or sit at the church's communion table. Regardless, these tables are connected, an expression of the same commitments and the same community.

'Injustice begins with forgetting,' McCormick says. This old, ornate table sitting at the centre of the church reminds me of this over and over again. It is a table connected to every table; the tables of Credo at the church's backdoor and the Verandah Café at its front; and other tables far beyond the church's buildings, those to which members of our community return each week once the Sunday service is done. At its best, the table of Jesus informs and implicates every table at which we sit, for it's a table of remembering and not forgetting, a table of connection not separation. Should we allow our church's tables to be places of forgetting, places disconnected from life beyond the church walls or secluded places of private spirituality, our tables will become nothing more than self-serve filling stations that ultimately gasp for spiritual breath.

There is a principle here as true for those who are religious as for those who are not, for all of those who value the health and vibrancy of our table life. The spirituality of the table is in the vitality of its connections, the free flow between our daily table routines and the expression of our values and commitments. It's in the business of remembering and not forgetting.

♦ RECIPE

Credo's Zucchini Slice

Tucked in the back corner of the Credo kitchen is a walk-in food pantry, home to a large refrigerator and lined with well-stocked shelves. What is striking when you wander in is as much what's missing in the pantry as what's there. To be honest, I had expected packets and cans galore, things pre-made and easy: open, mix and heat. But cans are rare at Credo. There's fruit, potatoes and onions in abundance, trays of fresh eggs and a colourful assortment of condiments and spices. Open the fridge and fresh vegetables are stacked alongside generous supplies of milk, yoghurt and cheese. While the Credo menu might be simple, this is no convenience store. Every day a dedicated team takes what's there and creates a healthy and generous feed for the fifty or so people who come.

Hidden away in the pantry is a nondescript blue book, stained and frayed at the edges, full to the brim with recipes carefully typed out and categorised: soups, mince and sausage recipes, fish dishes, egg dishes, rice and pasta, vegies, stews and casseroles, and desserts. There's nothing fancy in the book, but hardly any mention of cans or packets. Credo's menu has been a long process of experimentation – hits and misses, failures and successes – to figure out what works and what suits in a place like this. These are the stayers.

One of my favourites is Credo's zucchini slice, a simple eggy, cheesy masterpiece that makes the goodness of the zucchini palatable to those who would otherwise steer clear of anything remotely green. Served with a salad of fresh vegies and a simple dressing, it also looks great on the plate. Like everything on the Credo menu, this easy-to-make dish embodies the values of simplicity and care that so mark the Credo table.

The Communion Table

Ingredients
- 750 grams of zucchini
- 1 large brown onion
- 3 rashers of bacon
- 1 cup of self-raising flour
- 5 eggs
- 1 cup of grated cheese
- ¼ cup of oil
- Salt and pepper

Method
- Pre-set the oven to 170ºC and grease a medium-sized baking dish.
- Grate the zucchini into a large mixing bowl.
- After removing the rind, dice the bacon finely and do the same with the onion. Add both to the zucchini.
- Add the grated cheese, flour, oil, and salt and pepper.
- Lightly whisk the eggs then add to the mixture, combining everything well.
- Pour the mixture into the baking dish and cook for approximately 40 minutes or until nicely browned and set.
- Serve generous slices with a fresh garden salad. When I make it at home, my kids add spoonfuls of spicy tomato relish to give it an extra kick. It works!

CHAPTER 10

Conclusion
Eating Heaven

> *Whatever is genuine, whatever is real and true, thrives only if man does justice to both – ready for the appeal of highest heaven and cared for in the protection of the sustaining earth.*
> Martin Heidegger

The title of this book is *Eating Heaven*. Granted, it's an audacious one, but inspired in its audacity by Heidegger's words. It is a book offered out of the conviction that the shared table is an object of spiritual significance – that the practice of eating at it together is one that grounds us deeply in the 'sustaining earth' while always in reach of 'highest heaven'.

I cannot claim to know what heaven is. A professional failing on my part perhaps, but to me it is just one of many notions gathered up in the mystery of religious imagery. The traditional language of 'rivers of life', 'mansions with many rooms' and 'streets paved in gold' reads more like poetry than a descriptor of real estate. What I do know is that, firstly, heaven conveys a state of completion, an ultimate rest in which all of creation finds its fulfillment. As such, it holds relationship at its heart. Secondly, it is as much a descriptor of the fullness of life now as it is the hope of something yet to be: the sustaining earth and the highest heaven are not two separate spheres, but one. So, to claim that in eating together we might know something of heaven is perhaps not as audacious as it first sounds.

There are those who will argue with the premise of this book, and with good reason. The English writer Steven Poole is one of those. In his biting critique of the rise of 'gastroculture' in affluent Western societies, *You Aren't What You Eat,* Poole argues that to go in search of spirituality in food is at best to overreach, and at worst, 'a kind of perversity or decadence, an inward-turning dissipation of psychic and intellectual resources.' He is especially critical of the ascension of 'foodism' and the 'foodists' who worship at its altar, driven by 'a singular ideology' and who view the whole world through its 'grease-smeared lens'. As much as I could do without his sarcasm and misplaced caricatures of many very thoughtful table advocates, Poole places an uncomfortable finger on one of the great weaknesses of our current obsession, and especially of my pursuit of spirituality at the table. In the cultural and spiritual elevation of food, table life has been unintentionally diminished, rendered in completely self-serving and self-indulgent terms.

In a much more measured way, Rebecca Huntley makes a similar point in her critique of the Slow Food movement in Australia. In her book *Eating between the Lines*, Huntley contends that despite its founding philosophy that all food should be 'good, clean and fair', the movement has been sidetracked by 'food fairs, cultural tours, cooking demonstrations and corporate programs'. 'To be truly revolutionary,' Huntley argues, 'the movement needs to look beyond artisan-crafted goats cheese and address the needs of the most disadvantaged.' If we are truly committed to achieving nationwide access to food that is good and fair, Huntley says, we will work toward 'a republic of food in which everyone, regardless of social class, race or sex, is nourished and sustained by what Australia has to offer'. Instead, our pursuit of a purely self-indulgent table leaves us nothing but gastronomically constipated.

While willing to concede to Poole's critique of 'gastroculture' – a phenomenon as full of pomposity, food porn and self-indulgence as it is of goodness and beauty – I'll not surrender my argument that eating is a spiritual business or that the shared table is sacred space. It is so, in fact, for all the reasons that Poole, Huntley and others have identified. I hope that in the preceding chapters I have demonstrated, at least in part, that our life at the table plays host to some of the most important

Conclusion

aspects of what it means to be human and what it means to live a grace-filled life in community with each other and with the earth. Even more, I trust I have offered the beginnings of a case for a spirituality of the table that is found much more in connections, inclusion and justice that in boundaries, personal indulgence and excess.

A vibrant and life-giving spirituality is found in the congruence of heaven and earth, or, to use more pragmatic language, the point of intersection between our deepest values and the way we live our lives each day. As a person of Christian faith, for me those values are rooted in my encounter with God. For others they are rooted differently. Regardless, when those values are expressed in the way I sit at the table, when those values are allowed to forge connections between my life at one table and my life at another, I can confidently claim a spirituality of eating without embarrassment or excuse.

I began this book by describing my Friday ritual of breakfast at a local café: poached eggs on sourdough with mushrooms, and a strong flat white. It's been a while since I began this project, and though I am pleased to say my ritual meal remains unchanged – though in-season asparagus is hard to resist – my café of choice is gone. Sadly, too many cafés share a similar fate. It's a tough business. Regardless, I've moved on and up the laneway and the coffee is still good.

Though my café has had to change, the sustenance provided by this ritual is constant. It remains a spiritual practice for me, as significant and sustaining as any other routine discipline of my life. Could I do without it? Of course. I could survive without many things. Take away my laptop and my ability to write and I will live. Take away books and the opportunity to read and my life will go on. Take away my faith and my need to pray, and I'll still breathe. Take away my loved ones and friends and tomorrow still comes, though I can't imagine how. The fact is, the only thing we really need to stay upright is a certain mix of calories and nutrients, nothing more. But to what end?

It is through the daily practices of the table that we live a life worth living. Through the table we know who we are, where we come from, what we value and believe. At the table we learn what it means to be family and how to live in responsible, loving relationships. Through the table we live our neighbourliness and citizenship, express our allegiance to particular places and communities, and claim our sense of home and belonging. At the table we celebrate beauty and express solidarity with those who are broken and hungry. Some of us express our vocation at the table, the calling to create, to provide and to serve. At the table we initiate, welcome, celebrate, mourn, farewell, scheme, covenant, form alliances, and hope for reconciliation. At the table we tell our stories and listen to the stories of others, embracing difference, celebrating heritage and welcoming the stranger. At the table we express faith, confess our failings, remember our obligations and reach out for grace and community. Could we live without it? Yes. Would we choose to? No. For life without the table is no life at all.

References and Further Reading

Preface

Halligan, M., 'Writing about food: Ted Maloney, Johnny Walker, Leo Schofield, Peter Smark, Sam Orr and all', *Quadrant*, January 1977, pp. 16–19.

Chapter One: Introduction

Jung, L.S., *Food for Life: The Spirituality and Ethics of Eating*, Fortress Press, Minneapolis, 2004.

Chapter Two: The Kitchen Table

References

Huntley, R., 'White paper: "Because Family Mealtimes Matter"', Ipsos report prepared for Continental, March 2008.

Jones, M., *Feast: Why Humans Share Food*. Oxford University Press, Oxford, 2007.

Luard, E., *Sacred Food: Cooking for Spiritual Nourishment*, MQ Publications, London, 2001.

Further Reading

Avakian, A.V. (Ed.), *Through the Kitchen Window: Women Explore the Intimate Meanings of Food and Cooking*, Berg, Oxford, 1997.

Boyer, E., *Finding God at Home: Family Life as a Spiritual Discipline*, HarperSanFrancisco, San Francisco, 1991.

Busch, A., *Geography of Home: Writings on Where We Live*, Princeton Architectural Press, New York, 1999.

Gopnik, A., *The Table Comes First: Family, France, and the Meaning of Food*, Quercus, London, 2011.

Holt, S.C., 'Eating', in R.P. Stevens & R.J. Banks (Eds), *Thoughtful Parenting: A Manual of Wisdom for Home and Family*, InterVarsity Press, Downers Grove, 2001, pp. 107–112.

Krautkramer, C.J., 'Duty to cook: exploring the intent and ethics of home and restaurant cuisine', in F. Allhoff & D. Monroe (Eds), *Food and Philosophy: Eat, Drink and Be Merry*, Blackwell, Oxford, 2007, pp. 250–263.

Reichl, R., *Tender at the Bone: Growing Up at the Table*, Random House, New York, 1998.

Richardson, N. (Ed.), *Kitchen Table Memoirs: Shared Stories from Australian Writers*, ABC Books (HarperCollins), Sydney, 2013.

Seton, N., *The Kitchen Congregation*, Weidenfeld & Nicolson, London, 2000.

Visser, M., *Much Depends on Dinner: The Extraordinary History and Mythology, Allure and Obsessions, Perils and Taboos, of an Ordinary Meal*, Grove Press, New York, 1986.

Chapter Three: The Backyard Table

References

Berry, W., *The Art of the Commonplace: The Agrarian Essays*, Counterpoint, Berkeley, 2003.

Blainey, G., *Black Kettle and Full Moon: Daily Life in a Vanished Australia*, Viking (Penguin Books), Camberwell, 2003.

Dale, D., 'Around the tribal campfire', *The Age*, Epicure, 19 December 2000.

Duncan, C. & H. Giachin (Eds), *The Sustainable Table*, The Sustainable Table, Port Melbourne, 2011.

Fiske, J., Hodge, B., & G. Turner, *Myths of Oz: Reading Australian Popular Culture*, Allen & Unwin, St Leonards, 1987.

Gaynor, A., *Harvest of the Suburbs: An Environmental History of Growing Food in Australian Cities*, University of Western Australia Press, Crawley, 2006.

Halligan, M., *The Taste of Memory*, Allen & Unwin, Crows Nest, 2004.

Holmes, K., Martin, S.K., & K. Mirmohamadi, *Reading the Garden: The Settlement of Australia*, Melbourne University Press, Carlton, 2008.

Santich, B., *Bold Palates: Australia's Gastronomic Heritage*, Wakefield Press, Kent Town, 2012.

Saunders, A., 'Why do we want an Australian cuisine?', *Australian Cultural History*, no. 15, 1996, pp. 1–18.

Tsiolkas, C., *The Slap*, Allen & Unwin, Crows Nest, 2008.

Further reading

Kingsolver, B., *Animal, Vegetable, Miracle: Our Year of Seasonal Eating*, Faber & Faber, London, 2007.

Simons, M., 'Sustaining a nation: a river journey from basin to bowl', in J. Schultz (Ed.), *Griffith Review 27: Food Chain*, Griffith University, South Brisbane, 2010, pp. 13–30.

Thomson, M., *Meat, Metal and Fire*, Harper Collins, Pymble, 1999.

Timms, P., *Australia's Quarter Acre: The Story of the Ordinary Suburban Garden*, Miegunyah Press, Carlton, 2006.

Chapter Four: The Café Table

References

Brown-May, A., *Melbourne Street Life: The Itinerary of Our Days*, Australian Scholarly Publishing, Kew, 1998.

Clark, V. (Ed.), *The Parisian Cafe: A Literary Companion*, Universe Publishing, New York, 2002.

City of Melbourne Outdoor Cafe Guide, City of Melbourne, 2008.

de Certeau, M., *The Practice of Everyday Life*, trans. S. Rendall, University of California Press, Berkeley, 1984.

Dovey, K., 'On politics and urban space', in J. Barrett & C. Butler-Bowden (Eds), *Debating the City: An Anthology*, Historic Houses Trust of New South Wales, Sydney, 2001, pp 53–67.

IBISWorld, 'Cafes and Coffee Shops in Australia: Market Research Report', IBISWorld, n.p., 2010.

Jacobs, J., *The Death and Life of Great American Cities*, Random House, New York, 1961.

May, A., *Espresso: Melbourne Coffee Stories*, Arcadia, Melbourne, 2001.

Millar, R., 'Funky town', *The Age*, 4 June 2003.

Oldenburg, R., *The Great Good Place: Cafés, Coffee Shops, Bookstores, Bars, Hair Salons, and Other Hangouts at the Heart of a Community*, Paragon, New York, 1989.

Sartre, J.-P., *Being and Nothingness: An Essay on Phenomenological Ontology*, Methuan & Co., London, 1958.

Spurr, F.C., *Five Years under the Southern Cross: Experiences and Impressions*, Cassell & Company, London, 1915.

Wells, R., 'Need for a feed turns the tables on gloom', *The Age*, 17 September 2011.

Further reading

Allen, S.L., *The Devil's Cup: Coffee, the Driving Force in History*, Canongate, Edinburgh, 1999.

Bersten, I., *Coffee, Sex and Health: A History of Anti-Coffee Crusaders and Sexual Hysteria*, Helian Books, Sydney, 1999.

Boyer, M.-F., *The French Café*, trans. J. Taylor, Thames & Hudson, London, 1994.

Brown-May, A., 'Spilling the beans', in J. Barrett & C. Butler-Bowden (Eds), *Debating the City: An Anthology*, Historic Houses Trust of New South Wales, Sydney, 2001, pp. 229–39.

Harden, M., *Melbourne: The Making of an Eating and Drinking Capital*, Hardie Grant Books, Melbourne, 2009.

O'Brien, C., *Flavours of Melbourne: A Culinary Biography*, Wakefield Press, Kent Town, 2008.

Chapter Five: The Five-star Table

References

Bilson, T., *Insatiable: My Life in the Kitchen*, Murdoch Books, Millers Point, 2011.

Erlich, R., *Melbourne by Menu: A Memoir of Melbourne's Restaurant Revolution through the 1980s*, Slattery, Melbourne, 2012.

Farrelly, E., *Blubberland: The Dangers of Happiness*, University of New South Wales Press, Sydney, 2007.

References and Further Reading

Finkelstein, J., *Dining Out: A Sociology of Modern Manners*, New York University Press, New York, 1989.

Jung, J.S. *Food for Life: The Spirituality and Ethics of Eating*, Fortress Press, Minneapolis, 2004.

King, R.J.H., 'Eating well: thinking ethically about food', in F. Allhoff & D. Monroe (Eds), *Food and Philosophy: Eat, Drink and Be Merry*, Blackwell, Oxford, 2007, pp. 177–91.

Further Reading

Huntley, R., *Eating between the Lines: Food and Equality in Australia*, Black Inc., Melbourne, 2008.

Spang, R.L., *The Invention of the Restaurant: Paris and the Modern Gastronomic Culture*, Harvard University Press, Cambridge, 2000.

Telfer, E., *Food for Thought: Philosophy and Food*, Routledge, London, 1996.

Todhunter, A., *A Meal Observed*, Anchor Books, New York, 2004.

Warde, A. & L. Martens, *Eating Out: Social Differentiation, Consumption and Pleasure*, Cambridge University Press, Cambridge, 2000.

Chapter Six: The Work Table

References

Alexander, S., *A Cook's Life*, Penguin, Camberwell, 2012.

Bilson, G., *Plenty: Digressions on Food*, Penguin, Camberwell, 2004.

Chelminski, R., *The Perfectionist: Life and Death in Haute Cuisine*, Gotham Books (Penguin), New York, 2005.

Dinesen, I., 'Babette's feast', in *Anecdotes of Destiny*, Penguin, London, 1986, pp. 21–68.

Downes, S., *Advanced Australian Fare: How Australian Cooking Became the World's Best*, Allen & Unwin, Crows Nest, 2002.

Erlich, R., *Melbourne by Menu: The Story of Melbourne's Restaurant Revolution*, Slattery Media Group, Richmond, 2012.

Hearne, J., 'Hospitality: a cautionary tale', in J. Schultz (Ed.), *Griffith Review 27: Food Chain*, Griffith University, South Brisbane, 2010, pp. 80–90.

Huckstep, A., 'Foreclosure on a dream', *Food Service*, June 2008, pp. 28–32.

Mangan, L., *The Making of a Chef*, New Holland Publishers, Sydney, 2010.

Pépin, J., *The Apprentice: My Life in the Kitchen*, Houghton Mifflin, Boston, 2003.

Porter, L., 'Spice girl', *The Sunday Age*, 2 July 2006, p. 15.

Ruhlman, M., *The Soul of a Chef: The Journey toward Perfection*, Penguin, New York, 2001.

Symons, M., *The Pudding That Took a Thousand Cooks: The Story of Cooking in Civilization and Daily Life*, Viking, Ringwood, 1998.

Wright, S., *Tough Cookies: Tales of Obsession, Toil and Tenacity from Britain's Kitchen Heavyweights*, Profile Books, London, 2005.

Further Reading

Boulud, D., *Letters to a Young Chef*, Basic Books, New York, 2003.

Davis, D., *If You Can Stand the Heat: Tales from Chefs and Restaurateurs*, Penguin, New York, 1999.

Fine, G.A., *Kitchens: The Culture of Restaurant Work*, University of California Press Berkeley, 1996.

Ginsberg, D., *Waiting: The True Confessions of a Waitress*, Perennial (HarperCollins), New York, 2000.

Haas, S., *Back of the House: The Secret Life of a Restaurant*, Berkley Books, New York, 2013.

Holt, S.C., 'When it's an industry, what is hospitality?', *Zadok Perspectives*, no. 79, 2003, pp. 17–20.

Kelly, I., *Cooking for Kings: The Life of Antonin Carême, the First Celebrity Chef*, Walker & Co., New York, 2003.

Ruhlman, M., *The Reach of a Chef: Beyond the Kitchen*, Viking, New York, 2006.

Spillane, J.J., 'A Christian spirituality for hospitality professionals', in *People on the Move*, vol. 77, 1998, pp. 63–77.

Chapter Seven: The Festive Table

References

Ash, R., 'The taste of sad: funeral feasts, loss and mourning', in P. McNally (Ed.), *Voracious: The Best New Australian Food Writing*, Hardie Grant, Prahran, 2011, pp. 6–13.

Luard, E., *Sacred Food: Cooking for Spiritual Nourishment*, MQ Publications, London, 2001.

Santich, B., *Bold Palates: Australia's Gastronomic Heritage*, Wakefield Press, Kent Town, 2012.

Strong, R., *Feast: A History of Grand Eating*, Jonathan Cape, London, 2002.

Wirzba, N., *Food and Faith: A Theology of Eating*, Cambridge University Press, New York, 2011.

Chapter Eight: The Multicultural Table

References

Cook, J., *The Journals of Captain James Cook on His Voyages of Discovery*, Hakluyt Society at Cambridge University Press, Cambridge, 1955.

Farb, P. & G. Armelagos, *Consuming Passions: The Anthropology of Eating*, Houghton Mifflin, Boston, 1980.

Fisher, M.F.K., *The Gastronomical Me*, North Point Press, New York, 1989.

Flandrin, J.-L. & M. Montanari (Eds), *Food: A Culinary History*, Columbia University Press, European Perspectives, 1999.

Hage, G., Grace, H., Johnson, L., Langsworth, J. & M. Symonds, *Home/World: Space, Community and Marginality in Sydney's West*, Pluto Press, Annandale, 1997.

Nichols, D., *The Bogan Delusion: Myths, Mischief and Misconceptions*, Affirm Press, Mulgrave, 2011.

Shergold, P.R. & F. Milne (Eds), *The Great Immigration Debate*, Federation of Ethnic Communities' Councils of Australia, Sydney, 1984.

Shiels, J. (Ed.), *Cooking Stories*, Immigration Museum, Melbourne, 2003.

Soutphommasane, T., *Don't Go Back to Where You Came From: Why Multiculturalism Works*, New South, Sydney, 2012.

Zeldin, T., *An Intimate History of Humanity*, New York: Harper Collins, 1994.

Further Reading

McGinniss, L., *Feasts and Friends: Women and Food from across the World*, Freemantle Arts Centre Press, Freemantle, 2005.

Richards, E., *Destination Australia*, UNSW Press, Sydney, 2008.

Singley, B., '"Hardly anything fit for nan to eat": food and colonialism in Australia', *History Australia*, vol. 9, no. 3, 2012, pp. 27–42.

Symons, M. *One Continuous Picnic: A History of Eating in Australia*, Duck Press, Adelaide, 1982.

Wilton, J., & R. Bosworth, *Old Worlds and New Australia: The Post-War Migrant Experience*, Penguin Books, Ringwood, 1984.

Chapter Nine: The Communion Table

References

Brasher-Cunningham, M., *Keeping the Feast: Metaphors for the Meal*, Moorehouse Publishing, Harrisburg, 2012.

Karris, R.J., *Luke: Artist and Theologian*, Paulist Press, New York, 1985.

McCormick, P.T., *A Banqueter's Guide to the All-Night Soup Kitchen of the Kingdom of God*, Liturgical Press, Collegeville, 2004.

Neyrey, J., 'Ceremonies in Luke-Acts: The case of meals and table fellowship', in J. Neyrey (Ed.), *The Social World of Luke-Acts: Models for Interpretation*, Hendrickson Publishers, Peabody, 1991.

Further Reading

Bartchy, S.S., 'Table Fellowship', in J.B. Green, S. McKnight & I.H. Marshall (Eds), *Dictionary of Jesus and the Gospels*, Inter-Varsity Press, Downers Grove, 1992, pp. 796–800.

Capon, R.F., *The Supper of the Lamb: A Culinary Reflection*, Doubleday & Co., Garden City, 1969.

Koenig, J., *Soul Banquets: How Meals Become Mission in the Local Congregation*, Morehouse Publishing, New York, 2007.

Miles, S., *Take This Bread: A Radical Conversion*, Ballantine Books, New York, 2007.

Mendez Montoya, A.F., *The Theology of Food: Eating and the Eucharist*, Wiley-Blackwell, Oxford, 2009.

Jung, L.S., *Sharing Food: Christian Practices for Enjoyment*, Fortress Press, Minneapolis, 2006.

Symons, M., 'Did Jesus cook?', in Robert Dare (Ed.), *Food, Power and Community*, Wakefield Press, Kent Town, 1999, pp. 16–27.

Chapter Ten: Conclusion

Heidegger, M., 'The pathway', in M. Stassen (Ed.), *Philosophical and Political Writings*, Continuum, New York, 2003, pp. 77–79.

Huntley, R., *Eating between the Lines: Food and Equality in Australia*, Black Inc., Melbourne, 2008.

Poole, S., *You Aren't What You Eat: Fed Up with Gastroculture*, Scribe Publications, Brunswick, 2012.

Symons, M., 'Epicurus, the foodies' philosopher', in F. Allhoff & D. Munroe (Eds), *Food and Philosophy: Eat, Think and Be Merry*, Blackwell Publishing, Oxford, 2007, pp. 13–30.